The Cannabis Diaries

To Marie and Des

The Cannabis Diaries

a mother's struggle to save her family

Debra Bell

Appendix by Dr Zerrin Atakan

Hammersmith Press
London, UK

First published in Great Britain 2010 by Hammersmith Press Limited
82 Wandsworth Bridge Road, London SW6 2TF, UK
www.hammersmithpress.co.uk

Disclaimer
The central story in this book is the author's own but she has changed many names
to protect the privacy of the individuals concerned. The story is entirely from the
author's perspective and she acknowledges that her interpretation of the behaviour
of others may well not match entirely with their own recollection of events.
Furthermore, while the advice and information in this book are believed to be true
and accurate at the date of going to press, neither the author nor the publisher can
accept any legal responsibility or liability for any errors or omissions that may be
made.

British Library Cataloguing in Publication Data: A CIP record of this book is
available from the British Library.

ISBN 978-1-905140-30-5

Commissioning editor: Georgina Bentliff
Designed and typeset by Julie Bennett, Bespoke Publishing
Production by Helen Whitehorn, Pathmedia
Printed and bound by T J International, Padstow, Cornwall, UK
Cover image: 'Man walking Down the Line in the Road' © Bloomimage/Corbis

Contents

Foreword

I've been asked to write a foreword for these diaries because, from what I can understand, my story is integral to its content. I'd like to take this opportunity to give heartfelt congratulations to my mum (and indeed my whole family) that these diaries are now in print. I know, more than anyone, what a difficult, confusing and desperately unhappy time this was in our lives. This book is a testament to how powerful positive things can emerge from such darkness. It's a credit to my mother that she used these diaries not only as a coping mechanism for herself, but also as a tool to help vast numbers of people who were going through similar events in their lives. Everyone's story about cannabis, and its effect on family life, is different, but for most people the feelings are those of isolation, depression, anger and also fear for what the future might bring.

When I was in the midst of my admittedly very troubled teenage years, I concluded that every family had problems and that I was no different from any other person my age: I was experimenting with cannabis and just living my life. In a sense I was right. I was young, bright-eyed and eager to absorb as many different things as I could. I went to a large boys' independent school and a good friend was selling draw in class. I was 14. By the time I was 16, I was buying it regularly. It was all 'skunk' – there was no other type of cannabis available. I started smoking to get a buzz, to have a laugh and for recreation. Every party revolved around it. When you are a teenager, your friends are the most important thing in your life and I trusted them when they said that cannabis was harmless.

I had always been the 'good, eldest son'; my relationship with skunk was something my parents knew nothing about. I became reckless in my abandonment of the comfortable family life I had had. At the height of my smoking I was on about 12 grams a week.

Cannabis started to blur my moral lines. I began to steal from anyone, lying constantly to others and myself, and didn't seem to care, like it wasn't me who was doing it. Draw also gave me a shorter fuse, especially when I was coming down. I began to lose friends, and my family were at their wits' end – excluding me from the house, letting me back in – over and over again. It became a cyclical nightmare. In the end my family lost hope, giving up on me. Losing everything finally – friends and family – I had to start again by myself when I was still so young. I wouldn't want anyone else ever to have to go through that. To lose your family, especially, is one of the worst things that can happen to you.

Most of my school friends who smoked with me have had breakdowns of one type or another. Most accept that draw has a negative, depressing effect on them, although it varies massively from one person to another. That was confusing for me, for a long time, because I was one of the worst affected. I thought it must have been my fault, that there was something intrinsically wrong with me, not believing it could be the effect of skunk on my particular system. It became physically and mentally disabling.

From a parent's perspective you just hope that your child will stay safe, and that you have taught them enough for them to make the right decisions. However, when the train goes off the tracks and you begin to encounter more and more extreme situations, with the effects clear to see on all members of the family, then extremely tough decisions have to be made in the interests of protecting the family unit. These diaries I hope will be a source of comfort for those who have so many questions and very few answers. Most people have little support, apart from the help of friends who may mean well, but might not be able to relate in the way you need.

It's all very easy to talk with hindsight, though. When I was kicked out of home for the last time I felt my last strings of allegiance cut with my family and became unable to function as the person I once was. The thoughts, goals and ambitions of my younger self became totally unrecognizable to me. My living standards dropped from what I wore to what I ate. It took me a very long time to work out that the state I was in was not just my fault (I accepted all the blame and guilt laid at my door), but that I needed to make sense of what I had done. With or without my family I was also going to have to find a reason to live again. I worked out that through doing this I could eventually, maybe, be in a position to absolve some of the guilt that had brought me so far down.

I'm only 22 now, so I definitely have a long way to go in my life, and I'm still coming to terms with what happened to me. I can see now the importance of family and friends, of the need to tell the truth, to have self respect and to be as selfless as you can be. My heightened knowledge of these things, and my somewhat rebuilt life, can be used as testament to the difficult decisions my parents made. I can assure you though, that the pain of them practising 'tough love' with me was terrible. The anger and sense of abandonment were very real, and I still remember all of it to this day, but the reparations to my life thus far are probably because of those feelings – and the fear that I might ever have to feel them again. I no longer smoke cannabis and never shall now. I gave it up by myself, taking it slowly one day at a time, and I'm beginning to believe I may have a bright future ahead.

William Bell
2010

Acknowledgements

With many thanks to Georgina Bentliff of Hammersmith Press, and Suzanne Martin, for working so hard on these *Diaries*. I am indebted to Dr Zerrin Atakan, of the Institute of Psychiatry, for writing the medical and scientific information on cannabis which forms the Appendix of this book. Thanks also to Professor Robin Murray, for kindly introducing me to Dr Atakan. I am grateful to Sally Weale from the *Guardian*, and Lorraine Fisher of the *Daily Mail*, who helped me to go public with my story, to Jane Cunningham whose advice I'm so glad I followed, and to Stuart Swann for the website. It is impossible to name everyone who has supported the work of *Talking About Cannabis* since its inception, but I'd like to extend my thanks to all of you. Finally, without my wonderful husband and children none of this would have reached the light – my deepest love and gratitude.

Introduction

The diaries that make up this book represent just one year in the life of our family. It was a seminal year for us in many ways, starting soon after we had excluded our eldest son, William, from our home because of the impact his cannabis addiction was having on us all. He was 19. It was one of the lowest points in our family's relationship with him; all attempts to rehabilitate him into the family had failed. Yet he had started out as a boy of great promise and it was almost impossible to understand how we had come to find ourselves in this terrible situation.

William had been a highly academic, sporty, handsome, smiling and popular young boy who seemed destined for a successful life, but when he was only 14 he began smoking cannabis at his secondary school in South London. He soon began to change into someone we hardly recognized, who stole to fund the habit that began to consume him and us. He developed a chilling lack of conscience about the consequences of his actions, coupled with a frightening facility to lie and cheat. It was as if his soul had been sucked out of him.

Will had been a loving, responsible and outgoing child. He'd done well at school right from the beginning, and with the prediction of nine excellent passes at GCSE, we could never have foreseen that he would follow a route of drug abuse and destructive behaviour that would bring our family near to breaking point. Certainly the intensity of love that my husband and I had felt for our son when he was born contained no warnings that we would one day have to part from him in such a desperate way.

What had started as declining drive and ambition, coupled with petty stealing within the family, became truancy from school, deceit and in-discipline, both at school and at home, moving on to theft from others outside the family. It was clear to us that Will's behaviour over the pre-vious five years, which had gradually deteriorated, was not simply the product of teenage rebellion. For years, though, we were confused as to what was going on. Will was our first son, and it was 30 years since we had been teenagers after all. Society was changing faster than most of us could keep up with, and for a long time we presumed that what we were witnessing in our son was the result of normal adolescent changes for a boy of his time. We believed it was a phase and would pass.

When we realized that our son was smoking cannabis (after find-ing Rizla papers and small plastic 'baggies', with the remains of a foul-smelling herb, in his laundry), my husband and I were not overly concerned. We were surprised, because sport had always been central to Will's life, and we presumed – quite wrongly – that he would not compromise his fitness with tobacco or cannabis. He had begun using both at around the same time.

Our experience of cannabis was that it was innocuous, but our knowledge was out of date and when we began to look for help we were to discover that few members of our society took cannabis seriously, including the medical profession. Most of us were not up to speed with the fact that modern cannabis bore little resemblance to the 'bit of puff' or 'whacky backy' that our generation had used. Few people, other than users, knew what 'skunk' was. It was bewildering, especially as Will seemed to become increasingly dependent on it, and I wasn't even sure if cannabis was addictive. My distress calls to the Government drugs help-line confirmed this – cannabis was not physically addictive, was the message. Our son must be using a Class A drug, I was advised, because cannabis doesn't have the effects I was describing. Cannabis makes you withdrawn and relaxed, not aggressive or a thief. The ad-viser had not heard of skunk.

When I started writing these diaries, Will had been excluded from the family for two months, and was about to return to us. Three months later, we were to find ourselves organizing more permanent accommodation for him outside the house. There had been short expulsions before, from age 16 onwards, when he would go to a relative or to friends' houses. We had been trying for years to bring him to his senses, and help him change the behaviour that was turning his once-hopeful life into chaos. We had written down zero tolerance rules for the house, to put in place minimum standards of behaviour that would mean he could continue to live with us. These conditions included not bringing drugs into the house, not stealing, and not resorting to personal abuse of any family member. We had made the house and garden drug and smoke-free some months before. Seeing the rules written down in black and white helped us all; there was no mistake then if rules were broken. Sanctions were agreed with Will; interestingly, when they weren't followed through, and punishments were waived out of pity, Will would always 'up the ante', and his behaviour would get worse.

The whole family was suffering at his hands, and we could see it was particularly starting to affect our youngest son, Alex, who had been only nine years old when Will had begun to change. We became increasingly concerned about Alex and his older brother, Jack, and realized that we were in danger of failing to protect them. We knew that their memories of childhood could be wrecked permanently if we did not take action. Our health was at risk too. I was running on adrenalin permanently, as my body geared up for the next challenge. Being on 'red alert', I called it.

William decided to leave school after his GCSE exams, which we later found out he had passed, with good grades in some subjects. He decided to go to the local state-run sixth form college when term began again in September, but that summer more surprises were awaiting us. We went on holiday. Will had refused to come with us, and wanted to stay in London with a friend's family. While we were away, he broke into the house and large numbers of his friends followed. Coming back to the house after our holiday, it was hard to take in what we were seeing. The place was a sordid mess, with used condoms and evidence of drug use in the children's bedrooms. Every bed had been slept in. There was no sign of Will. This was very nearly a breaking point for us as a family because we could not agree on how to respond. My husband, Guy's, response was to write Will off, saying he'd never come to any good; he wanted nothing more to do with him. I felt a surge of anger against Guy. Will was our son, in spite of what he'd done; I couldn't harden my heart against my own child. I turned to tell my husband that if he carried on saying things like that, that would be the end of our relationship. Jack and Alex heard this, and were obviously very upset. They had had more than enough disturbance in their young lives; the house seemed to be constantly ringing with arguments between us and William. For their sake we had to hold it together.

Guy persuaded me that we needed to align as a family unit. We were both aware that William was taking up too much of our time and energy. He would come home after being away for days and, like a tom-cat, spray the house with his bad odour and then leave again. It wasn't fair on us as a couple, or on Jack and Alex. One thing I'm sure of now is that neither of them will ever do what William has done. They have seen and felt the pain it has caused.

We were in desperate straits by the time Will turned 17. His behaviour at home had escalated to intolerable levels. We couldn't believe a word he said; he couldn't even remember his lies, and would just shout louder and slam out of the house when challenged. If he didn't get what he wanted, usually money, he'd be beside himself. Once he slammed a door onto my hand when I was going through it to escape from his raging and trashing of the house, landing me in A&E. I didn't see him for three days after that. I was spending more and more time in tears, feeling frustrated, confused and angry. My husband was exhausted, working all day and then coming home to this nightmare.

William was eventually asked to leave his sixth form college; he had rarely turned up for class and had been stoned when he did. His main focus was on his next fix and getting the money to fund his lifestyle. We made it clear to him that if he was not going to do A levels, then he needed to get a job. He continued smoking weed though, but the house rules remained the same. William and Guy by this time were hardly speaking. My husband couldn't believe that this was happening in our family, and was furious with Will for refusing to address his behaviour. The summer before these diaries begin we found a flat for Will in

4

Streatham, and paid for the first three months, but he stole from us by forging cheques and pawning my jewellery to pay the rent after the first quarter was up. He never worked during this time; the flat was used to do more and more cannabis. He and his flat-mate (an old school friend who was also a heavy user of skunk) were asked to leave. My husband and I picked up the bills and paid off debts totalling thousands. The flat-mate's family was nowhere to be seen.

Will begged us to have him home again; he couldn't cope on his own, he said. He was still using cannabis, though, and was in a bad way. His teeth were stained a deep brown, his clothes stank of skunk and body odour. We considered his request to return and made it a condition that he go into rehab in the Priory Hospital first.

He did this. His grandmother paid the residential part of the fee; we footed the bill for the day-care afterwards. William returned to live with us, but within hours he had forged two more cheques from us, placing one of them into his own bank account – and the nightmare began again.

I had begun researching this drug on which our son had become so deeply dependent, when Will was around 16. I read that cannabis is the most widely used illegal drug in the world. United Nations reports showed it to be the most widely produced and trafficked illicit substance, and rising levels of seizures across the world suggested that output is increasing. The Executive Director of UNODC, Antonio Maria Costa, was issuing warnings that the make-up of cannabis was changing to be more like other plant-based drugs, such as heroin and cocaine. He raised the alarm about a cannabis pandemic, saying that it was becoming obvious that traffickers were investing in increasing the strength, and therefore the attraction, of cannabis.

Used by the 'flower-power' hippy generation of the 60s, cannabis became a symbol for the counter-cultural revolution of the time. There were demands by musicians such as the Beatles and Rolling Stones for legalization of the drug. Cannabis was seen as 'soft', 'recreational', and culturally more acceptable than any other substance controlled by the Misuse of Drugs Act, 1971. In 2004, cannabis was downgraded from a Class B to a Class C drug under the Act. The police were in favour at the time, yet three years later there were concerned voices in the UK. I listened closely when the Chief Constable of Merseyside was interviewed on television in 2007 about the appalling effects of cannabis on his community. He said that an elephant had walked into the room and no one had noticed. The elephant he was referring to was home-grown skunk cannabis, which I learnt comprised over 80 per cent of the cannabis seized on UK streets.

Derived from the plant cannabis sativa, the drug contains hundreds of chemicals. One of these is the psychoactive ingredient THC (delta-9-tetrahydrocannabinol), which causes the 'high'. Another chemical is CBD (cannabidiol), which may have anti-psychotic properties, possibly helping minimize the effects of THC.

Research at the Institute of Psychiatry in London was being published just as I was looking for answers. Professor Robin Murray was reported as saying: 'Five years ago 95 per cent of psychiatrists would not have said that cannabis causes psychosis. Now I would estimate that 95 per cent of them would say it does.' I began to panic and pleaded with our son to give up smoking the stuff. We were concerned that Will was indeed heading into full-blown psychosis. 'You may never be able to find your way home again after that; it can be for life,' I used to say to him. Meant figuratively in terms of Will's mental health, those words proved prophetic in a very literal sense, when a few years later we showed our son the door for the last time.

It was the house rules system, ultimately, that led to the permanent exclusion of our son. We always made sure, though, that he was not destitute: we arranged accommodation such as a flat, or bed-and-breakfast, or we organized for him to live with a grandparent. Our attempts to make our son see sense and quit cannabis were met with a shrug. Everyone was doing it, he would say, and he trusted his friends when they said it was safe. Will was 17 when the law was changed and cannabis was downgraded to Class C, although the seeds for this were sown some three years before when the Home Secretary announced that he was 'minded' to reclassify. The change in the law sent out the unspoken message that cannabis was safe, and semi-legal. Many young people saw it as a green light to experiment with it, and schools were confused too – most turning a blind eye to use.

Introduction

Our son and his cohort at school were all hitting adolescence just as all this was happening. When we found out that cannabis smoking among Will's group of friends had become the norm, we were horrified and angry. As parents, our authority had been undermined by the Government and when we looked for support and help outside the family, we could find none. No one was acknowledging an acute problem that we were struggling with on a daily basis. One thing I knew for sure: we were in the mire and feeling lost, therefore there must be thousands of other families like us who were going through something similar.

Unable to find support, I began writing an online diary which I published on a website I set up (www.talkingaboutcannabis.com), hoping to give comfort to other families who I knew must be suffering like us. After extracts were published in the national press, thousands visited the website and many of those people emailed me directly to share their experiences, which I posted on the site. The stories poured in, day after day. Most simply said that our story was also theirs. The players' names and circumstances were different, but there was one narrative line uniting us all.

Parents reported feeling they were to blame, just as we once had. Ashamed, alone and deeply wounded they strove to find an answer as they saw their child becoming more and more disturbed, often moving into violence and even suicide. Feelings of failure cause sadness, depression and marital instability. Sometimes parents part because they cannot agree on the best course of action. The pressure is too great. Other children in the family are then affected irrevocably.

It became obvious to me that cannabis and children do not mix; those who use it stand a high chance of being very badly affected. At best they will not fulfil their potential; at worst they may face a life dogged by mental illness. For every user, there is the family in the background, and most families get no support. Theirs is a private hell. Those people who would like to see illegal drugs decriminalized, like Professor David Nutt – the ex-Chair of the Advisory Council on the Misuse of Drugs – often use the argument that drugs only harm the one who is using the drug, so therefore it is wrong to penalize those individuals. This is not true. No one lives in isolation; we are all parts of units in so-

ciety and the main societal unit is the family. Families are all adversely affected by having a drug user in their midst; many are destroyed by skunk use in childhood. All societies have, and need, rules.

The general trend towards liberalization of drugs and the reclassification of cannabis in particular has undermined the family, leaving parents with little hope of a positive outcome for their children. It constitutes a betrayal of a whole generation, mainly boys, who seem to be the worst affected. We know that cannabis is fat-soluble and can sit in the fatty cells of the brain for up to 12 weeks in contrast to other drugs, like heroin and alcohol, which are water-soluble, and so are expelled by the body more quickly, often within hours. We know also that the brain does not mature until the 20s, so it is not surprising that Professor Murray and his team are finding that the risk of developing schizophrenia or psychotic symptoms is higher in younger cannabis users and those who smoke the stronger strains. His most recent evidence is about to be published. It will show that if you start using by the age of 18, then you are about one and a half times more likely to be psychotic by the time you are 26. If you start by 15, you are four and a half times more likely than otherwise to be.*

A parental action group was formed shortly after the huge response to the publication in the press of The Cannabis Diaries; this group later became a charity. We began a campaign to raise awareness of the 'hidden' problem of cannabis use by the young, urging the Government to change the law and return cannabis to Class B status. We asked too for a public health campaign to be delivered across the country, extending to schools and colleges.

The Advisory Council on the Misuse of Drugs, set up in 1971 to advise Government on controlled drugs, was asked to review the classification for cannabis again. (The Government had asked it to do so in 2006, and the Council advised that cannabis remain classified as it was.) The new review took place in February 2008. Along with another parent, I gave a presentation to the Council, on behalf of 'Talking About Cannabis', the Action Group, urging them to recommend reclassification back to Class B. Magistrates, mental health professionals and the

*Professor Robin Murray, The Report, BBC Radio 4, 19 November 2009

police all voiced their concerns on that day: that downgrading had had a deleterious effect.

The Advisory Council advised again that cannabis remain as Class C; the Government disagreed and changed the law once again in January 2009, reclassifying cannabis back to its original Class B status. The Home Office issued a statement recognizing the serious social and mental health effects that use of cannabis in childhood can have on families. This was a triumph for us and a step in the right direction, but too late to help Will and very many like him.

Debra Bell
2010

24 December

Letting go

It's Christmas Eve. This is the first Christmas that William has not been living at home. He is 19 and making a third attempt at A levels, by studying at a crammer in London, and now living with his grandmother, Caroline, in Surrey. We will see him tomorrow, when the family gets together for Christmas lunch at my sister's house, about 20 minutes away from here. Our other boys are now 16 and 13. The sadness and sense of unreality I feel at William no longer living with us is tempered by the relief that we have peace at home, something we have been seeking ever since our eldest son became a habitual cannabis user over three years ago.

We asked him to leave in October this year. At that moment I didn't care whether he ever returned. I knew we were doing the right thing for us all. As a family we had tried just about everything to help him, and still the madness was continuing.

Adored by all of us from the minute he was born, William was a good-looking boy, and became a loving, responsible and outgoing child. His brother Jack, two years younger, had given us concern, not settling easily into life. He had been an unhappy, often poorly, baby and child and had not enjoyed school at first. But Will had always had a sunny disposition, and had given us no cause for concern. 'You've got a smiley one,' a shop assistant once said to me motioning over to Will, who was grinning as he sat in one of those baby-walkers on wheels, trying it out whilst we were considering buying. I had laughed with her then, looking over at Will, and nodded in agreement.

Will was good with people, both adults and children, from early on in life and was of obviously high intelligence, doing well at school from the beginning, both in the classroom and at sports. He was ambitious too, and we presumed a successful life would create itself from these firm foundations. Our problems began when he started smoking tobacco at 14, the seemingly innocuous yet most culpable gateway drug of all. Soon after that, he started experimenting with cannabis with school friends.

Since he began smoking weed, William's main preoccupation has been getting hold of enough money to finance his lifestyle; he soon started stealing to fund it. During his GCSE year, his last year at school, money began to go missing from my purse and from his brothers' wallets. Portable CD players disappeared as did CDs, DVDs and PS2 games. Even clothes would go missing – presumably sold to buy dope. William would be mugged and have his mobile phone stolen every two months or so. Again, with hindsight, we can see now that all these things must have been sold for drugs. At the time I wasn't sure what was going on. He used to spend days away from the house; I knew very little about his life. Trying to run a busy household it's not always easy to see the bigger picture.

I never used to believe that William could have become a thief, just as I found it almost impossible to believe that he had become addicted to cannabis. I was unsure whether you *could* become addicted to cannabis anyway. I'd smoked some during my time at university back in the late 70s, and all it had done was give me the giggles; then I'd be asleep 10 minutes later. I didn't know that the stuff on the market now, a super-strength cousin called skunk, is very different, and smoking it as a teenager, when the brain is still developing, is highly dangerous. Mental health problems such as personality changes, psychosis and even schizophrenia can result.

As a family we have felt so alone these past years as we have struggled to cope with the changes taking place in our son. Because of this I have set up a support and information website called 'Talking About Cannabis'. I've decided to write a weekly diary for the site in the hope that it may help other families. This is the first diary entry. My hunch is that our story is not unusual; there are bound to be others affected. I believe there is a hidden epidemic going on among the young, and that cannabis smoking in the teenage years has become a norm. It's becoming accepted that drugs are in all schools, yet for every young person smoking cannabis there is the family in the background dealing with the potential fall-out. There is little outside support available, and little awareness of the effects of skunk on the young.

My husband, Guy, suspected that William was stealing from me, and so did I, but I presumed my son would admit he was doing this and then stop. Guy is a criminal barrister and I have sometimes felt that he has been too quick to see our son as a defendant in the dock. It has seemed to me that he wanted to write him off; labelling him a thief seemed cruel and insensitive. He was only 16 when this began – this did not seem the way to help heal the rifts between us and him. Money or property would go missing and my husband would immediately suspect William. I would say to Guy that we couldn't confront William directly because we had no evidence to support our assertions. 'What you're saying would never stand up in a court of law,' I used to say to him.

I was convinced that my way was the right way, and Guy's way wasn't. I found it impossible then to align myself with my husband's approach. Now I realize that the blend of our two approaches was a good one, but you must present a united front to your children. My belief then was that as long as you continued to be fair, and loving, you couldn't go wrong. I always thought with my heart and observed my husband's inability to do this towards William, secretly wondering whether he was jealous of our son now he was growing up.

William was by this time 6'5", an inch taller than my husband. They reminded me, at times, of two deer locking horns over who was head of the tribe. I loved them both, but so often felt in the middle of their wranglings, as though I was involved in some sort of personal loyalty test, which it didn't need to be. Instead of letting them get on with it though, often I would step in and try to make peace between them. Looking back, I see this didn't help. I have now learnt that I can step right back instead of forwards into the fray, and just let them sort it out. Certain things are not the business of the female; there are issues concerning the masculine that I can leave well alone. Boys learn to be men from their fathers, not their mothers.

In my attempts at fairness, when something went missing, we would often have a family meeting where both our other boys, Jack and Alex, then 14 and 11, and William, were asked if they knew anything about the missing property. Looking back, it would have been better to follow my husband's more black-and-white lead on this and say to William, 'I believe you have taken this', and then give a warning.

William always denied stealing from us, and a big part of me wanted to believe him. Over the years I have learnt to respond with a detached 'I don't believe you', when I know he is lying – and he is still lying a lot. Back then it would leave me feeling wretched and wrung out each time. I couldn't understand why he would want to take such a destructive path: drugs, stealing, raging, aggression – what was going on? Guy and I were both confused, and in shock. William had a privileged upbringing, in a stable family environment – surely he had no need to do any of this? I was hoping the nightmare would end soon; it had to.

29 December

Difficult decisions

We saw our son on Christmas Day. He and Caroline were driven up by my husband's sister, Martha, and family, who also live in Surrey, to have lunch with us at my sister's house in London. I've been wondering why I haven't felt in a celebratory mood at all this holiday. Something has been wrong, and it is of course because our son has not been living in our family. On his 19th birthday back in November, the first time he had not been with us on his special day, I experienced similar emotions. Feeling sick all day, it was as if he had died and I was grieving. Asking him to leave was another attempt to get through to him that we meant what we said about his behaviour in our house. It had become a matter of protecting the family: there are four of us and one of him. He had to go, and my secret hope was that the shock would be such a reality check that he would come back to us repentant. A supplicant bended-knees-type scenario was what I was hoping for!

So far, I'm still waiting for this last bit to happen. I'm still waiting for a spontaneous, genuine apology of any kind – forget the bended knees! William went to live with Caroline, my husband's mother, after spending the initial days of his exclusion from our house with a friend. He has a close relationship with his grandmother. She turned to me, though, before lunch on Christmas Day, to say that she thought William should be with his family. I've heard this before these past few weeks. She finds it impossible to accept that he is addicted to cannabis, saying that he's always been fine with her and that all he needs is tender loving care in the family unit. Getting her to accept how difficult things have

14

been for us is almost impossible. It's as if her brain doesn't want to accept the information, and just spits it back at us – almost as though, if she doesn't acknowledge it, it isn't happening.

My husband and I have tried to explain how destructive he is when he is with us, and how we have tried just about everything to attempt to modify his behaviour, at least in our own house. She listens but doesn't appear to hear. We're extremely grateful that she has allowed him to stay with her, but it is clear that she wants him to leave now and our first concern must be for her. She is 80 and, although extremely well physically, she is of a nervous disposition, and I am surprised she has been able to cope with her grandson for as long as she has. Even a 'normal' teenager would be stressful for an elderly woman unused to a young person in the house for any length of time. The responsibility has been too much.

My husband has always said that William will never live at home again, and I repeated these words to my mother-in-law on Christmas Day, feeling a sudden flood of liquid anger rise up from my gut, burning into my throat. She was shocked that I could be so cold-hearted ('How can you talk like that; you're his mother!'), and said her friends thought it disgusting her grandson wasn't with his family. She doesn't understand what we have all been through. Having William at home is like having a stranger in the house; it's been obvious for years that he doesn't want to be here. We tried setting him up in a flat earlier this year, so he could have independence but that was a failure; we are still picking up the debris from that episode. This has involved writing cheques for hundreds of pounds at a time to cover debts.

My husband has gone down to his mother's to collect William and bring him back home. I reported to Guy what Caroline had said to me on Christmas Day and after discussing it we decided that he could no longer stay with her. She seemed about to crack under the pressure, and that's not fair. Our first responsibility is to her, making sure she is well and happy, and William is our son after all. We offered to go and get him then, on Boxing Day, but it was agreed that he would come back today, Friday.

Every time I think about William being back here I get butterflies.

Some months ago we bought a safe to put all valuables and cash in, so at least we can put that system back in place. It is like inviting a burglar to live with you. I don't know how things are going to work out, but we have to take one day at a time; there is no other way to live.

31 December

Getting help

William is back in the house. Speaking to his father on the telephone whilst he was still at my mother-in-law's house, he made assurances that he was going to try '110 per cent' to make things work this time. Guy and our other two children went down to collect him on the 29th. I decided to stay at home. I needed some time to myself and also I wanted to get the house straight before he returned. Our priority has been to protect our property. We have locked away in the safe all cheque-books, and credit card statements. All my jewellery is in a pretty, but strong, box that my sister gave me for Christmas. It has a small, ornate golden key. Our bedroom door is now locked when we are not upstairs.

I was happy to see William when they arrived back, but I'm not expecting too much because past experience has taught me not to do so. We've had many new beginnings, all of them ending in failure. He looked pale and ill, with grey circles under his eyes. I'm always struck by the change in his looks since he became a cannabis user. Unlike his brothers who are fair, William is darker in colouring, with almost black curly hair and yet he has unusually blue eyes. His once olive complexion is now pallid; his deep blue eyes are tinged with red, the pupils almost permanently enlarged.

He went out with friends almost immediately he arrived back in the house, but these were old friends from his last year at primary school who were getting together for a reunion locally; one of them came to the house an hour after Will's arrival. I know that this young man neither drinks nor smokes and so he reminded me of a visiting angel, sitting as he was on top of a small chest of drawers when I went into William's room to say hello. I have been asking for a miracle after all!

After they left I went into William's room to draw the curtains, picking up litter that he had already begun to drop on his floor. Amongst the used bits of tissue and cellophane from cigarette packets was a familiar 'baggy'. Opening it to smell the remains of the weed it had held, I was glad I had decided not to become attached to any positive outcome. I'd been here many times before.

In May last year, during William's first attempt to do A levels (he was 17), about 10 minutes before we were about to leave for Spain on a Whitsun holiday I found around £300 in used £10 and £20 notes on a bookshelf in William's room. He must have heard me go into his room because he bounded up the stairs, asking what I was doing in there, pushing past me to slam his bedroom door in my face. I was getting used to this behaviour, but hated it. It was only a few months before that that he had slammed the front door on my hand as I was trying to escape from his raging, landing me in A & E. I was nervous around him now, not trusting that he wouldn't be violent towards me again.

Since he had been smoking dope he was always anxious to get as much money from us as possible. If he was thwarted over money he always lost his temper: shouting, slamming doors, being verbally abusive towards all of us. A large amount of cash in his room, though – this was something new. Asking him about it, he maintained that he had been working on a building site for a friend's father who had paid him in cash. We didn't believe him, and said so. Just about everything he said now turned out to be lies, which was stressful in itself. My husband told him that if the money turned out to be the proceeds of crime he would ask him to leave.

Another £400 in cash appeared in his room some weeks later. This money I banked for him. We presumed that this had come from dealing drugs; we couldn't think of any other explanation. I felt sick at the thought, and became very worried as to the company he might be keeping.

His conduct at home was becoming increasingly difficult to cope with. For example, if he wanted something, he would just take it. One afternoon I went to look for my mobile phone and spent over an hour searching for it, thinking I must have mislaid it, only to realize that William must have taken it. I was calm then, thinking that he would give it back when he returned, but that night was one of those where he had said he would return and then didn't.

I woke in the middle of the night, realizing that William had not come home. I was so angry with him – how dare he take my things? Being so furious with him, I got up to write about my unhappiness, asking myself how things could have become so awful. Writing is often the quickest way to calm myself, and to get answers. One of the things that I began to see when I wrote down my feelings was how very personal my phone was to me. If he had asked to borrow it, I would have agreed, but to take it without asking, how dare he...?

William had spent a lot of time over the previous few years staying with friends, frequently with his girlfriend who was an exceptionally beautiful, sweet girl, who lived with her widowed mother and two younger siblings on the other side of London. A virtual teetotaller, and vehemently anti-drugs, I couldn't understand how this young woman could find our son attractive, nor why she hung out with him and his friends who all smoked cannabis, but then again there were lots of things I didn't understand. (We found out months later that the cash I had discovered in William's room was stolen from this girl's mother, along with blank cheques from her account, which we found later in a stranger's wallet hidden under Will's wardrobe. By the time their relationship ended Will had also stolen from her younger siblings.)

His pattern was that he would come back, be charming to us for a while, in order to extract money from us (mainly from me, who he could melt very easily), then, once he had succeeded, he would go out promising to be back that evening, or the next day, saying that he would definitely text me to let me know where he had got to (another rule we tried to enforce to stop us from worrying as to where he was). Mostly, though, he would forget to text, and not come back until he'd run out of money. He would then return, shower, change his clothes and leave, and the cycle would begin again.

At first we would always try and track down where he was when he was away, but often his mobile phone would be switched off, and I wouldn't have landline numbers for most of his friends. In these days of mobiles, it's easy for wayward children to lie as to their whereabouts. We knew little about his life outside the house, and still don't.

Sometimes when I got to speak to him, he would sound stoned, then promise to be home but not show up for days. It would appear that we were the only household that didn't allow dope smoking, hence the reason he spent so much time away. He did smoke whilst he was here, though, and we would always challenge him about it. He didn't seem to care.

William had done well at school, winning a scholarship to his prep school, at seven, for academic excellence. At 11 he went to a large, well-respected, independent boys' school, about 30 minutes by coach from where we lived. Our youngest son Alex, 13, is at the same school now. Will was popular, and sporty, representing the school in rugby and football and was made captain of his football team. We'd go to watch him on Saturdays. He even became head of his school house. Things seemed to be going fine. He'd occasionally be bolshy and difficult, especially to his father, but we weren't worried about that particularly. To our dismay, in the most important year of school, he began to truant regularly and became increasingly rude and aggressive at home.

To obviate any confusion about smoking dope at home, we banned smoking of any kind in our house, including the garden. We also drew up a list of other zero-tolerance rules, even writing them down and all signing up to them. But within a few hours William had broken every one of them. I presumed this was all just particularly horrible, adolescent behaviour, until I started reading about the dangers of teenagers starting to smoke so early in their lives, when their brains were still forming. I began to panic, and feel really nervous for William, praying he'd stop doing it, come to his senses and get on with his school life. We'd always presumed he'd go to university with a good set of qualifications. But this wasn't to be the route for him or for us. His behaviour at home became worse. We couldn't believe a word he said; he couldn't even remember his lies, and would just shout louder and slam out of the house when challenged. If he didn't get what he wanted, usually money, he'd be beside himself, which is how I ended in A & E.

William decided to leave his school after GCSEs, saying he hated the place, and go to the local state-run sixth from college for A levels, starting in the autumn. He had passed all nine exams, some with very good grades. He took this as a sign that there was nothing wrong with what he was doing. That summer, though, as you know from the Introduction, worse was to come. He broke into our house when we were away and moved large numbers of his friends in. We came back to a filthy house, with condoms and evidence of cannabis use in the bedrooms; every bed had been slept in. I was virtually hysterical and couldn't believe my eyes. Will had left London to go to Cornwall with the family with whom he was supposed to be staying while we were away. I rang him immediately on his mobile, and screamed my disgust down the phone. He told me it was 'no big deal' and that they had tidied up before leaving – he could not understand my distress. We insisted he come back to London immediately, which he didn't. We had to go and collect him some days later from the friend's house.

Once back at home, Guy insisted that he write an apology to our cleaning lady and that he clean up his filthy room. We took away his door-key and grounded him for a week. But he refused to comply so we excluded him for seven days, during which time he went to stay with his grandmother. When he returned to London after that week, he left his bags by the side gate of the house and went out with friends, returning in the early hours.

William began studying for AS levels at the local sixth form college, and said he loved it. However, soon his teachers began to contact us. They were dismayed by him: he would regularly miss classes, and lie about why he'd been absent, often involving some elaborate deception. The college would then ring me and ask what the situation was. I was becoming increasingly frazzled, turning to my husband when he came home at night to ask him what we should do.

There was very little we could do, except to repeat to William what our expectations were of his behaviour in our house, and to plead with him to be sensible and stop smoking weed. We showed him newspaper articles about the evidence of links between psychosis and cannabis, particularly amongst teenagers. A friend lent us a video of a current affairs TV programme that outlined this new research that was coming to light. He refused to watch it, but appeared to listen as we spoke about our fears for his mental health and what we could see was happening to him. Telling us to get off his back, he would say that he would stop smoking if that was what we wanted, but didn't we know that the Government had downgraded the stuff so it couldn't be dangerous? We felt undermined by the highest jurisdiction in the land.

It had been a condition of William continuing to live in our household after he had been violent to me that we all attend family counselling sessions at our local surgery. I set these up immediately after the Christmas holidays, in January two years ago. Often William, then 17, would not turn up to the sessions. If he did attend, he would be in filthy clothes that stank of weed, often with urine stains down the crotch, his hair unwashed. He would shout at us in front of the counsellor, telling her that we didn't understand anything about him, we were inadequate parents who were out of touch with reality, and that his behaviour was normal for a teenager. The counsellor said she knew nothing about cannabis, which was very surprising to me. We live in an affluent leafy London suburb, but right next door to one of the most deprived inner city areas; surely her training would have involved some understanding of addicted teenagers? I didn't know then that family counsellors do not have drugs training.

Had William been abusing Class A drugs, I think she would have been alarmed, but she looked puzzled when we would bring the conversation round again to the effect cannabis was having on our son. 'Are you sure that is the problem? Let's just leave that for now, and look at what else it could be.'

After pressing her to consider cannabis as being a prime mover in the situation, she passed us on to a colleague of hers who was working at a drugs project in Lewisham. Finally, I thought we could get the help we needed. We waited three months for an appointment, and whenever I felt despairing I would reassure myself that the support we needed was just around the corner, and to hold on. Unfortunately, things didn't work out quite how I'd hoped.

William didn't turn up to the first session, so my husband and I spent a short time talking to the drugs counsellor, a young Scottish woman called Catriona. Apologising for our son, we agreed another appointment for the coming week. My husband could not take the time off work for that so I took my reluctant son down there alone, telling him that if he didn't attend this time he would have to leave. We walked there together, in the bright sunshine, or rather he walked behind me yelling at me most of the way, telling me I was a schizophrenic (a favourite taunt) and that it was me who should be seeing a psychiatrist, not him.

I felt so upset, hardly recognizing my son any more, my first wonderful boy who had been such a joy, not just to me but to everyone, when he was little. What had happened? Was it just the weed, or something else we'd missed? It had been a long time since we had had a calm, loving exchange, or even a laugh together. I would always be able to find my way back to forgiving him, though, and felt that if we could just get some help with his drug addiction, we might be able to cope and move ahead as a family.

The counsellor suggested she see William first. He told her that he had virtually given up smoking weed. I know this because I was called in after 15 minutes, when Catriona told me that my son was doing really well. 'He's virtually given up cannabis; he doesn't have a problem,' she said, smiling. He needed no help apparently.

Once we had left the building, William turned to me in the street, saying I was the one who needed help and that a professional had deemed him to be perfectly fine. We didn't see him for over a week after that.

6 January

All the tea in China

It's five in the morning and I've been awake since three. I decided to get up, make a cup of tea, and write down what is going around in my head, hoping that will help. I'm drinking too much tea. I'm not great with caffeine, but love both strong tea and coffee and the more I try to deny myself, the more I drink! When things are in turmoil I turn to things which comfort me. I know why – tea is a link to my mother, who died when I was 12. She was 39. Add a chocolate digestive biscuit (has to be McVitie's) and I'm even closer to her. We used to drink gallons of tea back then; she used loose PG Tips in a silver teapot, which lent a metallic taste to the stuff, but after two spoonfuls of sugar it didn't matter. Wonder what she'd make of our situation at home with the grandson she never met?

Need someone with a magic wand to get here fast. My youngest son, Alex, has bought me DVDs of the 1960s series *Bewitched* for Christmas, and we've been watching them together. He says they are uplifting, and that it's impossible not to feel happy when you watch them. Another link with my mum, too, before she got ill – I am about eight, and not long home from school. She's in the kitchen making our tea. I am lying on my tummy, crossed feet in the air, on the carpet in the lounge watching *Bewitched* (never realized the whole thing was in colour on TV sets in America). A safe time before she disappeared out of my life and nothing was the same again. Could do with a mother like Samantha's now to work a spell to 'fix' my son. Or my own mum would do, just simply to make me a cup of tea and tell me I'm doing fine. 'It doesn't take much to make you happy,' she used to say to me, smiling. Wish I could say the same for William. Sitting in my kitchen yesterday, I was discussing the website that I've set up with a friend over a cup of tea. (Another one!) She said how curious it was that I was trying to help other people when I couldn't fix my own situation at home. No, I can't. I've tried, but no can do.

William has only been back in the house a week, and I can hardly bear to look at him I'm so angry. I got upset on Sunday afternoon when I went into his room, which smelt strongly of tobacco, to find him lying, unwashed, in an unmade bed watching television in the clothes he'd been wearing for three days and nights. I've been asking him not to go to bed in the clothes he's been wearing all day since he was 11. I've also been trying to get him to make his bed for the same number of years. There was ash on his bedside cabinet. He knows the house is a smoke-free zone, so what the hell is going on?

There was rubbish on the floor and food stains on the new carpet, which we had already had to replace this year due to cigarette burns and the rest. Feeling an upsurge of anger when he refused to make his bed ('No, I won't, so just go away!' he shouted), I replied by spitting out the words that I couldn't see things working out here if he was going to be like this.

'You'll just have to find somewhere else to live, if you can't follow the basic rules of the house that we've been talking to you about for years!' I yelled, knowing I was over-reacting, but years of the same exchanges get to you in the end.

'Is this your idea of 110 per cent effort?' I continued, going into spiteful-mother mode, blindly picking up clothes from the floor and throwing them onto a chair.

I flounced out, telling him to obey the rules or leave.

Guy and I had a meeting with him later, downstairs in our living room. I was wound up and just wanted William out of my life. Guy became the referee, and calmly took over. We both said we wanted things to work out here, how we loved him but would not put up with rudeness and flouting of the basic rules of the house.

'You do understand we both want this to work out this time, don't you?' Guy said, kindly.

William replied that he believed his father did want that, but that I didn't. What? Oh, this was new, and I silently celebrated that at least here was something, because these two had hardly spoken for months – make that years. Maybe I needed to get angry for that small bridge to appear between them out of nowhere. I smiled inwardly. Hmm. I looked over at Guy and could see a softening, as he took in what his son had said. I decided to let him do the talking, whilst I tried to subjugate my feelings of wanting to kill someone. (Guess who?!)

He began talking to William about how getting his A levels this year would be such a boost to him, how from there he could decide what to do.

William must be at one of the most expensive schools in the country – just under £6,000 a term. Guy's mother is financing it; it was her idea, actually. She's always been generous with money. After Will had been in rehab in the summer he expressed an interest in going back to school, and she said she'd pay if he wanted to go to a private place. It's an immense amount of work though; he is doing three A levels in one year. He is obviously struggling between wanting to drop out and smoke weed for the rest of his life, and his realization that this is his last chance. It is a miracle that he is still there.

After Will had left the room, Guy told me I mustn't immediately talk about him having to leave because it wasn't helpful. If he forges cheques again, or steals, then of course that's different, but not for smaller things. I know he's right, but started whining, saying that this is my life too, what about me? I calmed down later and went upstairs to hug William, asking him if we're cool. As he hugged me back, uneasy feelings surfaced because I don't remember a time when he's ever come to me to apologize, unless it's been to then ask me for money. It's always this way round. He's never even apologized for the big things he's done – like pawning my jewellery or forging my cheques, or injuring my hand. We've always insisted he say sorry, but it's never felt genuine.

I'm scarred by what we've been through, but he doesn't seem to care, as if his conscience was taken away by cannabis. We know he's still smoking; he told us that by bringing an empty 'baggy' into the house. My husband termed it a 'two fingers up' to us, but William did his usual trick of saying it was months old.

His behaviour at this new college has been similar to the last two attempts at going back to school. Suspended twice last term, he is now on a threatened expulsion, for repeatedly lying to tutors and bunking off. He has to attend every class for the first two weeks of term, and only a doctor's note will suffice as an excuse, or he will definitely be expelled. We believe that as long as he is smoking weed, he won't be able to cope with this sort of a course. I have told the college enough about William's past difficulties for them to be able to deal with him appropriately, but not in such detail that they will immediately throw their hands up and ask him to leave.

His personal tutor, Suzanna, lurches between compassion and frustration. We know that seesaw well. His end-of-term report included phrases from teachers such as 'deceitful', 'elaborate lies', 'coming to class worse for wear' and 'no work ethic'. The contrast with his school reports up until the time he was a habitual cannabis smoker is blinding.

We talked to William about making a good start to the term. 'I'm not stupid, you know. I know I need to get my A levels,' he said, looking down, tears in his eyes. Of course, he knows. So, it's over to him. We can't live his life for him.

A new term began the next day for William and also for Jack, who is 16, two years younger, and now in the lower sixth at a local comprehensive. But, what's this – it's 7.30 am on Day One and William is saying that he's not going in? I smile, trying to calm myself, and say I'll drive him to the station. ('Get your things together. Of course you're going. You're on a suspended expulsion.') He said he was ill, and had been up all night. Guy went into his room and told him to get up, reminding him that he was watching TV until the early hours, so he would be tired, but he needed to go. Guy and I looked at each other. I couldn't believe this – the first day back.

I managed to get William into the car with me somehow. He was moaning, saying how ill he was – no one ever took him seriously, not like we did with the other boys. I said that he could blame us for everything, but it was still his future he'd be mucking up. Arriving at the railway station, I watched as William placed a finger on the door lock, pressing it down, refusing to get out. Dizzy with rage, I then remembered that he needed a doctor's note for any absences and drove him to our local surgery. William was shouting at me all the way. I remarked that for someone who was ill he was able to shout loudly enough.

I hate these comments I come out with, but I don't know what to say or do any more. He was still shouting as he got out at the surgery, and slammed the car door. Oh, God, let this not be happening.

Feeling stronger by the time I got home, I rang the college and told William's personal tutor that I thought he was faking, but that if he could convince a doctor he would present a note when he next went in. He returned an hour later to spend the day in bed watching TV, and sleeping.

He was ready for college the next day.

'The doctor diagnosed it,' he told me, without looking me in the eye. 'I've got stomach problems. I mustn't eat carbohydrates after six. I got a doctor's note, so it's all good.'

He was in the kitchen, energetically cutting bread and cheese to make sandwiches for himself. I glanced over wearily at the pile of washing up. His dishes along with everyone else's. Off all yesterday and not even a cup washed up by him.

I asked him if the doctor also recommended he eat an entire packet of chocolate biscuits? (I had bought McVitie's, couldn't find them and asked Jack, this morning; he disappeared into William's room whilst he was in the bathroom, coming out with an empty packet, apart from two left at the bottom. My biscuits!)

'I didn't eat all of them,' William replied.

'Oh, that's right. You left two,' I said. 'Did she also recommend you eat chicken tikka at 11 o'clock at night?' I was getting nasty again.

'Well, I had to eat something.'

William had refused dinner with us last night, choosing to come down later when we were going to bed.

I told him that I didn't believe he was ill. He called me a bitch, then, saying I'd done nothing to make him feel welcome since he had come back to the house, and then slammed out. We didn't see him for two days after that.

He is back now. Presumably he's run out of cash. I can't even look at him. He hasn't apologized for being rude, which will be because he thinks I was rude to him for not believing he was ill. I don't know where we go from here. I can't do this for much longer. I have butterflies in my stomach almost permanently, as my body gears up for the next thing, I suppose. Neither Guy nor I sleep properly any more, nor have we for several years. Jack recently said, 'I can't have all this shouting when I'm trying to do my A levels. It's not fair.' Our youngest son, Alex, 13, just retreats to his room, or becomes extra nice to us both; he also over-eats. I don't know – I wish I could fix things, but I can't. I'll have another cup of tea instead.

15 January

Peace breaks out

One of the worst weeks of our family life last week, but this weekend saw a breakthrough of sorts, and yesterday, Sunday, was the first peaceful day we have had as a family for many years. Phew… It's a Buddhist way of life we're leading – having to take each day as it comes. We never know quite how the day is going to play out, so staying in the present moment is all you can do. Mostly I don't remember to do this, and race ahead in my thoughts – and lose myself. I got a surprise this week, and last week too, when Jack, and then my husband, reminded me, individually, that living in the present moment was the only way we were all going to get through. I've talked about 'living in the moment' for so long, and now if I forget I get reminded by the very people I've been trying to convince, which is wonderful.

So much has happened over the last week, and I hardly know where to start. I've also been sitting on a jury for the past three months, on a money-laundering case, which shows no sign of finishing, so time is short.

The weekend before this one I thought I was going to have a stroke I was so angry with William. I just couldn't see how this living arrangement was going to work. Sick of having to lock everything valuable, including keys to the house, inside the safe in our bedroom and then lock the bedroom door too, resentment was building fast. If I could have seen that he had any sense of wanting to make things right again with us, that would have helped. But he seemed not to care, and obviously didn't want to be here. On Sunday afternoon, I felt at my most crazy. By

Sunday night, as worse began to unfold, I looked back at the afternoon and wished I was there again!

William had been out on the Saturday night, returning on Sunday afternoon looking ill and pale. He was obviously stoned. His eyes were dead-looking, with the familiar large dilated pupils, and dark shadows beneath. He had asked to borrow Guy's phone on Saturday (he has lost his own), but had failed to return it. Guy asked him, when he returned, why he'd taken his phone out of the house without permission from him, and why he couldn't have sent a text to say he would be out all night, to let us know. William shouted abuse at his father, and then shut himself in his room. I followed him up there later having an urge to wash all his clothes, most of which were dirty.

Taking his jeans off a chair, emptying pockets of tissues and other rubbish, I found in there a silver handbag mirror which I recognized as belonging to Caroline. We had given it to her as a gift not long before. Will was lying on the bed watching TV. I asked him what it was doing in his pocket. I remembered that he had been wearing those trousers when he returned from his grandmother's to live with us the week before.

'It's mine,' he said, looking at the mirror. 'Let's have a look? Oh yeah, I'll have that.'

'No, you won't,' I said. 'It belongs to Grandma.'

'No, it doesn't.'

There was also a small bag in his jeans which had obviously once contained jewellery – earrings presumably. 'Oh, that's a Gucci fake. Worth nothing,' was William's response. Later, after William had gone out I opened his school-bag and found what could only have been stolen property in there – a mobile phone and a Marc Jacobs, diamond-studded man's watch. Hardly believing what I was seeing, I checked the phone, and left a message for the person who owned it, telling them to contact me. My husband then telephoned Caroline and asked her to check if she was missing a silver mirror; she was. He told her about the other goods we had found, and she expressed her disbelief.

Challenging William about the things we had found, he said that they weren't stolen and friends had given him both the phone and the watch. He said he could explain everything if we gave him a day to do so. I spoke to the owner of the phone the next day, who said that the phone had been 'lifted' from the table where he was having lunch in Pizza Express on the South Bank on 21 December. That was the day I had invited William and his grandmother to have lunch with us, to celebrate Alex's 13th birthday – at that same restaurant. Jack and I had taken Alex and two school friends up to London to meet Will and Grandma, who had arrived ahead of us. We must have all been there when the theft had taken place! I began to really fear for William's mental health now. Thinking about it later, I became convinced that William was having a breakdown, something I knew was a possibility as long as he continued to smoke weed, because he had begun so young.

The question remained – what to do now? Guy confronted William with what we had found out about the stolen phone the next evening, when he returned home at around midnight. He quickly lost his temper as Will began denying stealing anything.

'You brought stolen goods into our house – get out! You're a thief! How dare you bring stolen property in here? You're no longer my son, and I want you out of here!' he yelled.

Alex was in bed, and began crying, saying that he didn't want any more shouting. I went up and got into bed with him, holding him tight. I could hear Jack march into Will's room, telling him he needed to get help, that he was a drug addict and couldn't he just get a grip of himself and admit it. Will was shouting and crying, saying he had nowhere to go, whilst Guy called 999, to tell them about the theft. They didn't come, but an officer rang the next morning at around 8.30 to say they would be there within the hour. I wanted to ring the court to say I would not be coming in for jury service that day, but Guy told me to go, and he stayed to wait for the police. They came mid-morning and Guy gave them what he had found, saying that he wanted to get the goods out of our house. William was lucky not to have been arrested. So far we have heard nothing more from the police.

When I got back from jury service that day, Jack told me that Grandma had rung for me. We later found out that William had rung her that morning, telling her that he was going on a holiday after his AS exams and could she give him £300. In spite of being told by us the night before that we had found her silver mirror in Will's pocket, she promptly, with no reference to either Guy or myself, went down to the bank and transferred £250 into William's account. When Guy rang her, after receiving Jack's message that she had phoned, I heard him asking what on earth she was thinking of by giving Will money only 12 hours after she had heard that he had not only stolen her property, but also that we had found stolen goods in his bedroom.

Guy told her that he found what she had done a betrayal of him – that we were trying to get Will to modify his behaviour in the house and that giving him a large amount of cash would not be helpful in trying to get him back on the rails; it would just go on drugs. I've never heard Guy so angry. He feels that his family have taken William's part too readily, believing what Will says despite what we might tell them.

We have made it a condition of William remaining here that he get help. Thousands of pounds have been spent on rehab therapy over the past year, and so the treatment he gets from now on is going to have to be on the NHS. He and I went to see the GP this week, and I have found a place where he can get free help – a Community Drugs Project in Forest Hill. We have been this route before with a Drugs Project in Lewisham two years ago, but the difference is that William is now saying that drugs are ruining his life, and that he will seek help and go along to the drugs counselling. His first appointment is next Saturday.

Since our discovery of the stolen property, William's behaviour has been much better at home. He has talked and cried, and said how sorry he is – for the first time sounding genuine. Maybe this is the 'rockbottom' that people have told us he may need to reach before he comes 'up' again. I don't know. What I do know is that we had a peaceful day here yesterday, with us all together as a family. We took a walk through Greenwich Park down to the river, and I can't remember the last time we did that. Present moment stuff, where you just rest in the peace and hope…No, I mustn't hope about tomorrow. No attachment to any outcome. All we can do is just enjoy the moment, taking one day at a time.

1 February

Changes

I'm no longer sitting on a jury. After three months the trial has collapsed, so I'm free. Hurray! It felt strange on Friday, saying goodbye to the other 11 jurors, knowing that having spent hours together every day since November last year, we would almost certainly never see each other again. I am now at home, blowing dust off the life I had before.

Will is here all day too. His personal tutor, Suzanna, with whom I've had conversations almost daily, rang me last Tuesday – a much looked forward to day off from court – to say that Will had been sent home and that almost certainly he wouldn't be allowed back. She sounded tired and bored by the whole thing, feelings I know well.

The college has had enough of him. They don't want to deal with a student who lies so easily, doesn't turn up to all his classes, and when he is tackled about what is going on lies again (only this time louder), getting aggressive if he is crossed.

'He just doesn't seem to care and never says sorry. All he's got to do is tell the truth, but his lies are damaging and we have to think about the impact on other students,' I heard her say.

She told me that Will had been playing tutors off against each other, and I guessed she meant that she had been personally hurt by this, and asked her if that was right. She said yes, and sounded sad. The reference to other students was also because she had been called by another student's mother the week before, saying that she thought Will had plans to stay at her house again that weekend and she didn't want that.

Will has been sleeping at friends' houses for over three years now, and it's always worried me that he might be annoying people, so it was almost a relief to hear that a family was complaining.

Having been suspended three times before, we had received a 'final warning' letter about William's behaviour at the end of the previous week; quite simply he had to turn up to every class and be punctual, or he would be expelled. There was reference to the way he looked too. I know I should be ashamed, but I'm past that. The day the letter arrived, Will was not at home and returned in the early hours looking awful. I let him in, and told him about the warning, and that the letter was on his bed. The next day, resisting the desire to scream at him to get up, I woke him at the normal time, then left for court hoping he would have the good sense to go in. He didn't.

The college is excluding him now, with a view to his returning in September. I asked for a meeting to try to convince them to keep him on, if only to salvage something for the large fees we have paid. You'd have thought the huge investment that's been made on his behalf by his grandmother would have informed his behaviour; you'd have thought...

Guy said he didn't intend to persuade the college of anything. He felt that they wouldn't be interested in what we had to say and rightly so. I told his tutor that I thought Will was very ill, and having some sort of breakdown. She's been very calm and helpful throughout.

Will had an appointment at the Community Drugs Project in Forest Hill the next day, Saturday. As you know, I had taken him to the GP the week before to get some sort of help, making two appointments, one for each of us, so we could have a little longer with the doctor. We saw a locum, who was pleasant to us and recommended we self-refer to the local drug counselling unit in the borough. This must be new, better than last time we asked for help. Guess things must have moved on in two years. The GP gave me some numbers to call. I rang them immediately I got home, and spoke to a drugs worker called John, at somewhere called the Dual Team in Catford. I got more out of my call to him than I had out of months of speaking to Will's doctors at the Priory last year!

I told him about Will's lack of concern for others, his destructive behaviour, how we have now had stolen property brought into the house, how Will had told me the day before that when he steals he gets a rush. 'Oh dear, oh dear, you must be very worried,' he said. He had a comforting voice, deep, with a soothing West Indian accent. He was listening to me, and seemed to know something of what I was relating – I had waited a long time for this. He began to tell me about the effects of cannabis, or indeed any drug, on mental health and moral outlook.

'The things that you and I would find a turn-off, they find a turn-on. That's what your son will mean by the rush when he steals. How much has he been smoking do you know?'

'He's told me that it can be around five spliffs a day sometimes, and at others not so much, but he still smokes every day, I think,' I said.

'Right, well, he needs to come off it for the sake of his mental health. What happens next is that the voices come in, and I wouldn't wish that on any parent. But I would refer you to the Community Drugs Project; the people we have here are much older than your son; their lives are in chaos – a lot have serious drug- and alcohol-related illness too.'

He then gave me his hospital mobile number, telling me to phone him at any time. This was quite incredible, and gave me a lot of strength.

On Saturday Will saw a counsellor named Sally, and seemed to like her very much, saying she was 'jokes'. Maybe some seed for the future here. Guy and I waited for him in a small coffee shop around the corner, and afterwards we took him for breakfast in a greasy spoon next door to the drug place. Will had had a girl in his room the night before (we had heard the front door go at around seven in the morning when she left) just to add fuel to the fire of not turning up to college that day when he'd been on a final warning. I guess having a girl in his bed might be considered normal behaviour for a 19-year-old, but Will just seems deliberately to up the ante with us. He knows he's not allowed to sleep with his girlfriends in our house; he has no privileges because of the way he's been. You'd think he'd want to get us on his side; you'd think…Guy talked about that in the greasy spoon, as Will tucked into a bacon butty, telling him he needed to have his sex life elsewhere. Oh God, why can't we just have a normal family life, whatever that is, a bit of peace and quiet as Guy would say? We had a difficult conversation with Will; he told us that life had never been easy living with us, and that we had been very strict parents. Guy and I took this as a compliment. He also seemed to have a new insight that his stealing is his way of self-harming. I presume this piece of wisdom must have emerged from his meeting with his new counsellor. Hmm, that's interesting. Yes, seeds for the future, I can feel it. I let Guy do most of the talking, and just observed the two of them. We all agreed that Will needs to keep up his appointments, and he seemed genuine about that.

We have had a peaceful time since then, on the whole. Will has seemed relaxed. He is no longer under pressure at college. 'Living a feckless life,' Guy is calling it, and he's probably right. After a meeting between us and the college, it has been agreed that Will can continue on a very restricted timetable, probably only two hours a week, with an individual tutor, to complete his ASs, which will mean that if he wants to continue to A2 at any time he can. He's been at home with me all week, and seems very different. Almost certainly he has stopped smoking weed and for the first time I feel that the worst may be over; I know it is. He's been asked to go into college to meet his new tutor tomorrow.

Not such a good sign was Will preparing to go out for the evening. Guy has predicted that he won't be able to get up and won't go in, and shouted at Will, telling him just that and that he shouldn't be going out. Will did go out though, saying he'd be back by 11. He was meeting his new girlfriend, a young woman who lives locally and with whom he was at primary school. The same one who left the house in the early morning the week before.

'Why does he need to go out the night before he's due to go back into college?' Guy really began building up after Will had left, accusing me of not being with him over this ('as usual'), even though I had said I didn't agree with it either.

'I can't stand him being around, everyone dancing attendance, when he's a liar, a cheat and a con-man. It won't be long before I'm throwing him out again, I can see it. I can't wait. I'm sick of all this. I loathe him.'

Of course he's sick of it, but I wish he could flow with the changes a bit more. I told him tonight that I loved him more than anything else in the world, but there are such huge changes happening here, and I know that Guy finds it difficult to cope with change – as we all do. I'm doing alright with it, because I have seen it coming, and I'm happy to embrace it. Now that Will is no longer acting out, I know that the other family members will feel that, and respond, sometimes in a negative way. Alex has become very bossy, and Guy is angry and confused, expecting a return to bad behaviour at any moment. He is a lawyer, and makes predictions based on historical precedent. Many times he has been right, but I can see that there is growth happening here for all of us. I need to be more compassionate with my husband, but also I need to remember that I don't always have to be the peacemaker in the family. We are all going to feel the change in different ways, but one thing is certain – that we are all growing. That is the gift in having a child like Will. And maybe that is what we are all here for – to grow, not to stagnate. I talked to Guy about this, but he seemed unconvinced; he is in a lot of pain.

I can, however, let Will and Guy work out a new relationship with each other; it has little to do with me. I am myself trying to rebuild one with my son, and it's not easy. I'm very nervous around him, expecting him to be unstable and flip out at any moment.But we've had over a week of good behaviour from him; without weed he is so different.

Guy and I went to bed tonight not talking. He was so angry about Will going out, and I didn't know what to say without getting angry and spiteful too. He began to lose it when I agreed that Will could wash the car at dusk to make some money, calling it a waste of time doing it in the dark. I was amazed he wanted to make money instead of stealing it!

I woke up at 2 am with a noise from Will's room. Getting up to write this, I realized that Will has his girlfriend in his room again, and found a ripped-off piece from a condom packet on the landing. Guy is going to go crazy when he finds out in the morning. Will's bedroom door was ajar, just to add to it all. I went to close it, not particularly quietly. I just hope Will goes into college, and doesn't prove his father right. Wish me luck.

17 February

'Fool, if you think it's over'

I did something last week that I rarely do. I bought myself a new CD – *Chris Rea's Greatest Hits* – and now, as I sit down to write, one of his songs comes into my head: 'Fool, if you think it's over'. His music reminds me of the late 80s when I was working in documentaries for BBC Bristol. We were filming in the US and the cameraman, who had become a good friend, bought me one of Rea's CDs. Listening to his music again takes me back to simpler times.

Maybe I was a fool to think the worst was over with William. I'm upset with him again. This week I did something else I don't normally do and bought myself a DVD, of the movie *The Da Vinci Code*. It went missing before I'd taken it out of its HMV bag. I'd left it in the study and then couldn't find it. I asked everyone at home if they'd seen it, and today, days after it had disappeared, I decided to look for it properly. Puzzled as to where it could have gone, I found myself standing in Will's room, looking at his white drawstring bag, and found the DVD in there, its plastic bag crumpled underneath it, the receipt alongside. Will is not here, having gone out last night and not returned. I guess he was planning to take the DVD back to the shop and get a refund on it. A small thing, you may think, but it's cumulative. We've had repeated incidents like this over the years and have made it clear to Will that it has to stop, and now it's happening again.

Alex has just told us that his new mobile phone has gone missing too. We have gone over when it was last seen, and have concluded that Will may have taken it with him when he left. Guy is furious, saying that Alex must look after his belongings, as we have a thief in the house. 'It's a hard lesson you have to learn, I'm afraid,' he told him. Alex had tears in his eyes as he responded to this, saying that he wants to be able to use his things without locking them away all the time. I explained to Alex that we are all upset that this is happening again. Jack has just come in too and is dismayed to hear my news about the thefts. He says Will needs to get some new friends because of the pressure to smoke when he's with the ones he has.

'He goes looking for people who smoke, though, I think. So many people smoke now, but none of my crowd – we think they're idiots,' he says.

He's just returned from a gig in Brixton, and starts to tell me about a man he saw who was handing out Es right in front of him.

'One of the guys who took one started to look really ill and had to leave. His eyes were awful. They're crazy. You okay though, Mum? About the Will thing, I mean?'

I tell him I'm fine, just upset obviously. He says goodnight to me, leaving the room murmuring about making sure everything's locked away.

We still put all our valuables in the safe in our room. Am I going to have to put any purchases that Will may take a fancy to in there as well? Just wondering how we're going to continue like this, beginning to trust a little more because Will seems to be more 'normal', and then a nasty surprise waiting. There was also a message on the answering machine today for Will, asking why he had missed his counselling appointment this week, and was he returning? Yes, he most certainly is. We've made it a condition of him remaining here that he gets help. He'd told us that as it was half-term there was no appointment. That, it would appear, was a lie. More old patterns.

I took him on Monday to attend his appointment at a local mental health centre, from where there may be the possibility of a referral to the Maudsley Hospital. His behaviour had continued to be good at home over the previous three weeks, until now, since he stopped going into college every day. It's not been easy for me, having him in the house all the time, but I've been aware that he needs to rest and recover from three to four years of sleeping on other people's floors and doing massive amounts of cannabis. I have said nothing to him about his getting up at noon and doing very little for the rest of the day. We have re-written his CV together, though, and he has been applying for jobs.

He had been looking much better. I never got used to him looking dirty and ill. He has let his hair grow now, is showering regularly, and generally wearing clean-ish clothes. He seems genuinely to care about making good our relationship, but is smoking again. On Sunday, the day before his appointment with the psychiatrist, he came home having obviously been smoking weed with friends. He was ill, clutching his stomach, saying he had pains. His pupils were wide, too. (Suppose I should have been suspicious when little bottles of eye drops started to appear in his room these past two weeks.) He slept all day. A repeat of this happened on Tuesday too. So, weed is back on the scene – hence the stealing, I suppose.

On the way to the clinic, Will started to tell me he didn't want to have to tell his life story again to another doctor. I told him that every time you tell it you see yourself a little differently and that that, in itself, can be very useful. I tried not to start gabbling, which is what I do when I get nervous, picking up on his tension. I remembered reading somewhere that a winning duo is to think quickly and speak slowly. Well, sorry but no can do.

The Mental Health Centre was housed in an old Edwardian house in a sought-after residential area, just off the main road that leads from Lewisham to Bromley. Steep steps led up to the front door with its peeling grey paint. As we entered the waiting room I clocked the 'No Smoking' sign, yet the room smelled strongly of trapped tobacco smoke. Tugging upwards at one of the double-glazed windows was not successful, so I sat down again. Fraying grey chairs were laid out in a horseshoe shape. There was a series of small posters on one wall, warning of the dangers of drugs misuse. A couple in their thirties were waiting too, one of them on crutches. The woman began coughing, that familiar sound that can only be produced from smokers' lungs, and fumbling in a pocket she began to pump something noisily from a tube, inhaling melodramatically.

Will didn't seem to notice, and turned to look at me, telling me that all he needed was a job to get his life back on track. He didn't need any more therapists, so why couldn't I understand that? I asked him if he wanted me to stay and wait for him, and he turned his head away, mumbling that leaving him with a load of doctors would be just wonderful. The irony is that I had sat in that same waiting room myself about 12 years before, and I'd lay money on it that it hadn't been decorated since. The windows definitely hadn't been opened. It was not long after my third son had been born.

Each time I had had a baby, I had begun wanting to know about my own early years, and become aware that there was a void in my life that I didn't know how to fill. I had had four years of Jungian therapy in my twenties, but after Alex was born I had been to my GP about the possibility of getting some help with the bereavement scars that I carried. She had suggested I go for a short course of CBT therapy at Guy's Hospital, but I needed to get referred first by attending this clinic. And here I was again now with my son, who at the time I had come here before had only been a small child of seven. Oh my, how things turn out. However, I know that sadness and depression can be a gift, because they can lead you to an understanding of yourself that you would never have had otherwise. You really can heal your life, and I'm a classic example of someone who has done just that.

Will returned from seeing two trainee doctors, and I could tell a change had taken place because his eyes seemed much bluer. Maybe the eyes really are the windows to the soul, and soul-work is most certainly what was going on here for Will. To tell your story, seeing your words paint living pictures of your experiences, is to access the soul. And it's hard work. Will was starving and we walked out to get a quick breakfast at the local greasy spoon, before Will saw the consultant.

When we got back a new patient, a man in his early forties, had arrived in the waiting room. We heard him tell the receptionist that he was breaking down, and needed to see someone right away. He then paced the room, repeating what he'd just said to her. I kept my eyes on my book, but wished I could help in some way. Will returned after an hour with the consultant, who then invited me to come down to talk to her.

Well, this was new. Will said he had asked her to see me. Really? That's great, I thought. I walked downstairs to a small room where the consultant and two student doctors, in white lab coats, were waiting. I wished I'd gone to the loo, though, before being called down. If I'd known... my one chance to get some sort of diagnosis of Will's problem and I'd had a cup of tea on top of a bottle of water.

The psychiatrist was a woman in her fifties. Her jaw-length, grey-flecked bob looked as if it might have once held one of those black velvet alice bands that were popular in the 80s. She was wearing a long, flouncy denim skirt that had seen better days, thick tights with court shoes and a single string of pearls around her pink turtle-neck sweater. She was very friendly and began to talk to me about my son, who had elected to wait outside. She agreed that he was undoubtedly troubled, and could benefit from psychotherapy. He had told them, however, that he was happy to continue with the counsellor he has at the moment, and didn't want another therapist.

'It's a bit like you've brought him in for an MOT, you see,' she explained to me, smiling.

She told me that he was not suffering any major mental illness, that he didn't need medication, and that maybe getting a job was what he needed, although she wondered whether he would be able to be disciplined enough to keep one. He had told them that he had had a trial day at a job, which I explained was not true. They all look confused. I assured them I was right on this.

We talked and she agreed that he could be referred to the addictions unit at the Maudsley, which is what I told her we should like, and she said she would arrange it. Will could decide which route he wanted to take when the appointment came through, she said. I felt happy with this, and Will seemed upbeat too, but was probably just relieved to get out of there. I felt the same. Another experience we have survived together.

24 February

If this is the road to hell, let me get out of here

After a difficult weekend a week ago, Guy and I have had two serious rows this weekend already and it's only Saturday night. I'm so tired.

Getting off this rollercoaster with William would be nice, but how to do that? I've been coping with having him at home again every day this week by helping him get a job, but now I'm feeling wrung out and empty. We made a list together of what needed to be done, which included signing on to get Jobseeker's benefit, and sending off as many applications as possible to get a temporary job, while he is still doing what has turned out to be a one-hour weekly class at college.

You will remember that a new DVD had gone missing and also Alex's mobile phone. We only discovered later that Jack's iPod had also been taken from his room. Will arrived home late last Sunday afternoon. I had put on my DVD and begun tackling the overflowing ironing basket whilst I watched it. I ironed most of the day. It always makes me feel calmer if I'm ironing. I find it grounding and soothing. When I'm feeling upset, putting washing in the machine or ironing always helps. I do a lot of both as a consequence!

Guy had been working upstairs most of the day. He was due to begin a three-week fraud trial in Sussex the next day, and had preparation to do. As usual when things are blowing up at home, he is about to be in a black hole, out of town, leaving me at home with Will. It's happened too often to be coincidence; we've both remarked on it, and it worries Guy. I guess he must remember well the day he came home to find me with my arm in a sling, after Will had shut my hand in the front door whilst

I was trying to escape from his raging.

With Will back from wherever he'd been, Guy came down and asked me if I was ready to talk to our oldest son. Nodding, I looked over at Guy and could see he was tense and uneasy. I'd begun being both things the moment I had heard Will come into the house. He had gone directly up to his room as normal. Guy called upstairs to ask Will to come down into the kitchen to talk to us, like we've done scores of times before. I could hear Guy asking him to sit down as we had things to discuss.

Walking into the kitchen I hadn't realized quite how furious I was with him.

'Where have you been for two days without letting us know, and why did you steal my DVD? I found it in your bag. How dare you help yourself to my stuff? I guess you were going to take it back to HMV to get the money back, weren't you?' I said, feeling my breathing go out of synch.

Most of the time I can find a loving space within me to deal with my son, but just then that seemed securely blocked. Looking over at Will I could see he had tears in his eyes, and his face was going red like it always used to when he was little and about to cry. He was looking down at the floor, arms and legs crossed. I wanted to be something else with him, yet all I could feel was anger verging on hatred, and utter frustration that we were having yet another conversation about stealing. All I wanted then was for him to leave so we didn't have to do this any more. He said he had taken the DVD to play at a friend's house. I said I didn't believe him.

'I'm so hurt you could do such a thing, after all the other things you've taken of mine over the years. You've had my jewellery. You've forged my cheques. You knew I was looking for that DVD. I asked you if you'd seen it. Do you remember? When you were doing ironing to make some money and you said you hadn't seen it? I just don't understand how you can do that!' I was definitely in my childish lower self now.

'And what about Alex's mobile phone? Where is that?' Guy began. 'You know how precious that is to him. He's only just got it. He's been looking for that all over the house. I will not have my other children upset because of you, do you understand? Do you?'

Will said that he had replaced Alex's phone, back in Jack's bedroom where he'd borrowed it from.

'I just borrowed it for a text, and then realized I'd taken it with me later on. I didn't steal it. I just borrowed it. I don't have one so I borrowed Alex's.'

Guy explained to him it wasn't borrowing; it was stealing.

'You go off yet again not telling us where you are, not letting us know you're not coming home, not even giving us the courtesy of a call when you had a phone. How can we go on living together if you're going to start behaving like this again? Can't you see we've all had too much of this? I've told you before, this family comes first. There's four of us and one of you. If you upset your mother and your brothers you'll have to go,' he said.

I looked over to see that Guy had started to peel vegetables for dinner. He was going at them vigorously and shaking the potato peeler at William as he then went on to explain his view that when he's on dope he steals, and he's got to stop smoking. I joined in saying that he had been smoking since he was a very young boy and we're seeing long-term effects here.

'It's ruining your life – can't you see?' I said.

'That's right. I'm useless,' Will shouted. 'Here we go again – you two bringing me downstairs to tell me what you think of me. Great parenting that is! I've had this since I was 14. You telling me it's all down to cannabis, when can't you see, it's the way you treat me that's the problem. You're always threatening to throw me out. Brilliant that is – makes me feel really wanted. I'm happy with cannabis now. It just isn't an issue. I hardly smoke at all, so it can't be the problem, but you can't see that. If you knew just how much everyone else smokes and they don't fuck up like I do, but you won't accept that.' Then he walked out, yelling, 'I won't sit here and hear you blame cannabis.'

I went upstairs to see him later, after I'd calmed down and ironed every garment in the house. I felt able then to put my arms round him and give him a kiss. He told me how confusing it was when I'd said only the week before that I was enjoying having him around now that his behaviour was so much better; I obviously hadn't meant any of it. I explained that I had meant it, of course I had, but now I was angry because he'd taken my stuff yet again.

'It's "and...and", William,' I explained. 'Yes, I was enjoying having you around. Your behaviour has been much better and I was happier with that, and now you've stolen from me and I'm angry but it doesn't mean that what I said before was untrue. It's both things – "and...and". Can you see that?'

He said he could but that his life was just so awful he couldn't see the point of any of it. I explained to him that we needed to get him to see the drugs counsellor the next day, that we could send lots of CVs off and really make a stab at his getting a part-time job if that was what he wanted. ('You know it is, Mum.')

The next week was better, despite Jack realizing on Monday morning, as he was about to leave for school, that his iPod had gone. (Oh no, surely not that as well?) Jack asked me to check in the safe where he thought his father had put it for safety. When I told him it wasn't there, he told me that he thought it had gone, but that he would have a better look for it later; now he had to go to school.Will was still in bed and didn't get up until midday. I went in to his room to ask him about it, telling him that we needed it to be returned if he had taken it, and could he replace it please if he had. It turned up in Jack's room later that day.

I spent most of the day on Monday, the day after our showdown with Will, trying to talk to the psychiatrist with the pearls that we had seen the week before, with no luck. I wanted to update her, and see if we could get some urgent attention for Will. Guy and I had also decided that we probably needed to try and sort out somewhere else for Will to live – that maybe we could look to him moving out and into a flat by the end of March, so we needed to get things moving now. The psychiatrist had told me that I could speak to the social worker attached to the clinic at any time, and they could help with finding Will accommodation if we needed it. But now that I wanted to enquire about exactly that, I couldn't find anyone to help me. I spoke to a nurse at the clinic who told me that I should try to get a social worker for the family, and to ring the town hall to arrange it.

How depressing. I couldn't bring myself to do that, believing anyway that they probably have much worse cases and wouldn't take seriously a middle-class family living in a nice neighbourhood, where the father was a lawyer and the children attended private schools. Instead I encouraged Will to make an appointment with his drugs counsellor, Sally, which he did, making it for Thursday. As it was only Monday, I phoned her back and said we had had a difficult weekend where things had been stolen from the house and that Will needed to see someone urgently. She said she could see him later that day, and I drove Will over there.

Will did not want to go, telling me that drugs weren't a problem so why did he need a drugs counsellor? I told him that stealing other people's belongings was not normal behaviour and he needed to get help with this.

As we drove over there I began reminding Will that he needed to talk to Sally about the stealing – which he had once told me was like kleptomania, and a 'sort of schizo thing' with him. We had had a good conversation that day; it was when he was in rehab at the Priory last summer. I was visiting him, which I did every day. He had a room overlooking the gardens at the back of the hospital, and I was sitting next to him on his bed looking out at other patients who were walking round the grounds. There was a young man with headphones kicking a football by himself.

I'd been telling Will about the research that shows that teenage cannabis use often leads to schizophrenia, and he had nodded, saying that it was happening to him in a small way already. We talked about the party we'd given at our house for his grandma's eightieth birthday, to which he'd been invited. We'd all been pleased to see him. (It was at the time last year when he was living in a flat in Streatham, for which we were paying.) Whilst we were singing Happy Birthday, Will had been upstairs stealing jewellery from my room. He had taken an antique ring, which he later gave me back, and a specially designed necklace that Guy had bought for me shortly before. Insisting he take me to the jewellers where he'd sold it, I was told when we got there that they had melted it down for the gold. Only just holding back the tears, I told them that that piece was mine. Didn't they think to ask where it had come from? When I asked them how much they had given my son for it, they said £20. The piece had cost over £200.

Almost a year later here we were again, talking about the same problem.

'I take things because most of the time I don't feel alive at all. And when I take stuff it's only then I feel alive. Nothing goes right in my life, I just muck everything up. I've messed up college again for the third time. I can't get a job. I've been trying for three years and no one wants me. What's the point?'

I glanced over at him. His eyes were closed, his head resting on the door of the car. Oh God, what do I say here? I felt wretched that my own child should feel this way about his life, and that I can't seem to help him. I know he needs to get help, and Sally is all we have at the moment. At least he is agreeing to go, so that has to be a positive. He's so vulnerable and yet so difficult to deal with; there's an aggression there. It's like he's a stranger yet he is my eldest son. There must be a way through this if I can remain strong.

7 March

Stepping back

I'm taking some time out. I've driven down to the Dorset coast, and checked into a hotel overlooking the sea. It is quiet and beautiful here, more so than I remember it being from when I came here with Alex last year. I am alone on this occasion, the first time I've taken any time away from my family that has not been a business trip, and never for so long. I plan to stay four nights. I have a double room to myself, with a sea view, for which you have to pay extra. The Grand Hotel is perched on a cliff top in Swanage, with a private beach below that you reach by means of a steep wooden stairway. There are palm trees in the garden, and little tables where you can have tea in the summer. Looking up I can see that a large family of doves has moved in just below the rafters, behind the large faded letters spelling out the name of the hotel. After last night's heavy rain I'm surprised to have woken up today to a searing sun reflecting its glory onto the sea, in the exact same spot as the moon was the night before. How magical that is; I wish I knew more about the moon and why, unlike the sun, it cannot always be seen and certainly not in the same place two nights running.

After being, at first, almost unable to sit down from worrying about what I should be doing, I am now getting more used to being able to do exactly what I want. My adrenalin levels have been running danger-ously high these past few years. I guess it will take more than a drive down the M27 to slow them down to a normal rate. It's often only when you relax that you realize just how stressed you've been. I am still wak-ing up, though, and going to bed too, thinking about William, with even more reason now. He is no longer at home. We placed him in temporary bed-and-breakfast accommodation last weekend.

I think I'm trying to say that we threw him out. Again. The strain of locking doors, worrying about property going missing, wondering where he is, waiting for the next call from his college about absences – all of this was beginning to be too much. Guy is still working on the trial down in Chichester, choosing to commute from our home in South London, and as a result is almost catatonic by the end of the week. Weekends are prime sorting-out-problems-with-William events. He usually disappears on a Friday. We are never sure where he is, or whether he'll be coming back – small beer you're probably thinking considering his behaviour over the years, but it's the smallish things that, when repeated, get to you most.

After spending a lot of time with the computer and telly, both going at the same time in his bedroom, and sleeping in his clothes, Will had a sudden rush of energy that seemed to come on after a trip to the Job-centre to sign on. He went for an interview at a restaurant in the City, and returned triumphant, saying that they'd offered him a trial shift the next day. He could go to his class at college in the morning, and then on to the job. I gave him a hug and said well done, and the next day gave him money for a travelcard and food, and off he trotted, clean and besuited. Jack was convinced that his brother was telling the truth this time, and remarked to me how he seemed to be excited by the prospect of working. Will didn't call to let us know how things had gone, nor did he return that night. When he came back on Saturday he told me that he'd been paid by cheque for the work he'd done at the restaurant, and that the manager had told him to ring in later, to find out if he'd be needed that night.

It all sounded plausible, but it wasn't true. Something made me ring the restaurant the next day (Will had given me a name). Will, meanwhile, was again sitting at computer/television, when he wasn't sleeping the day away, fully clothed. One thing was clear: he had not been invited back to work there. The manager I spoke to had never heard of him. Another lie. He hadn't been into college on Friday morning either, the only morning he is invited into the place now.

So, talking to Guy on Sunday morning, we both decided that it was time William lived on his own. Constantly lying to us was almost as bad as stealing from us. He hadn't been to his drugs counsellor either, and only went when I took him there. Still in his dressing gown, Guy came out of the front room with the Yellow Pages in his hands saying he had an idea he'd been thinking about. He sat down at the kitchen table and started to ring local bed-and-breakfast places. None of the ones advertised could help, but he was put on to an Italian family who take in paying guests – Mario and Maria. Yes, they could take him, they said. Today would be fine. And that was it; we had somewhere for him to go. Last time we'd asked him to leave, back in October, when we found dope in his room again, we had left him at the local railway station at 10 o'clock at night, giving him a hundred pounds to go. I'd spent the next three days worrying about him, until I found out he was at a friend's house and perfectly fine. At least this time we'd know where he was. It seemed simple enough, even though the whole thing was ghastly and depressing – a given for us. Jack said he wanted to go to the gym, so I gave him a lift – popping into the supermarket on the way back for potatoes. Guy was planning on cooking a roast for lunch, so we could eat before throwing out our son. Hmm. Looking forward to that.

While I was out, Guy woke William, packed up his clothes and told him he was going to have to go, as we'd all had enough. No bended-knees supplication from Will, I was surprised to see when I returned. I just don't get it; I would never let anyone put me in a B&B. I'd have done anything to make sure I wasn't sent away. But not this one. He doesn't seem to feel he has the power to make the changes in his life that will lead to peace for him or for us. He sat in his coat, refusing to eat, and played the piano while we all ate lunch.

Guy insisted I come along to take William to his new place, although I felt ill at the thought. Alex told me I should do it for the sake of all the family. The house was in Catford, part of a long grey row of other identical Victorian properties, amid several miles of similar-looking intersecting streets just off the South Circular. You could so easily get lost here; all the roads looked the same.

I couldn't bring myself to go into the house, and stayed in the car, but I got out to give Will a hug, telling him to look after himself and to call me. Guy took him in and came out smiling, saying how nice the Mario-Marias had been.

'They're lovely,' he said, as he started up the car, looking relaxed. 'She's like Bella Lasagne out of *Fireman Sam*. She's a real maternal type, really sweet; you'd like her. He'll be fine there. It's not as if we're sending him to a household like the Wests' place.'

Oh, great! You mean they aren't likely to cut him up and put him under the patio? Good one. I did smile, though, when Guy told me that William would be sleeping under a picture of the Madonna and not the one that sings! Let's hope this works out. Guy says he's almost sorry for Mario, but had handed over £160 in cash, and that had made him smile. He didn't leave our home phone number. Wise move. At the very least it would give us a Will-free week, but as to the long-term future, that was undecided. Guy's plan was that Will apply for housing benefit that week, and then he could be re-housed at a later stage.

The next day, Monday, Will rang me up at 11 o'clock to ask if he needed to vacate the house during the day. He'd just got up. I reminded myself that this was another reason he needed to be away from us. He liked to spend his days in a semi-vegetative state, and being in someone else's house I'd thought he might not feel he could do so. It appeared I was wrong about that. Even though we had asked him to leave, I did not want to give up on Will. The next day I went to talk to a GP about the fact that I was convinced more and more that Will had become ill through his addiction, and my concern was that he was heading for psychosis and schizophrenia. I explained that if someone could convince Will that he was suffering from an illness that would not go away by itself, he might be able to avoid worse problems than he had already. The doctor told me to bring Will along and he would do what he could.

I took Will along with me on Thursday, but the meeting did little to help. I challenged something Will said, which was a lie, and he got very angry with me and began shouting at me in front of the doctor, turning to him to say, 'Can you see what I've got to put up with?' The doctor told me that the way I was talking to my son was dysfunctional. As I tried to explain why I'd challenged my son, he told me he wouldn't listen to anything more I had to say and began smiling down at his folded hands, shaking his head. I left them to it, which was probably what I should have done from the beginning, knowing though that if I did there would not be a positive outcome. Which there wasn't.

I left Will at the surgery and drove off at speed, unsure where I was going, but ending up at the shopping centre at Bluewater, half an hour away. I cried all the way. I wasn't sure I could do any of this any more. I just didn't have the strength. I was trying to help him, but I don't think he really wants to be helped, which frustrates the life out of me. And now someone was telling me I'm dysfunctional when all I want is for my son to get better.

Will disappeared the next day, without letting the Marios know where he was, which upset them. He was due to check out of the B&B by 10 o'clock the next Sunday morning. Guy and I decided not to organize another place for him, seeing as he'd gone without telling anyone where he was. We went to collect his things when there was still no sign of him on Sunday. He turned up there again late that evening, wondering where all his stuff had gone. When he rang our house, Guy told him that he was on his own now. The conversation went on for some time.

Everyone I've spoken to lately has said that we have to step back and let our son reach the holy grail of 'rock bottom', from which he'll then come up. So, that's what we've done and it feels awful. I hate not knowing where he's sleeping. He rang me as I was sitting down to a large cappuccino in a café on the promenade today. It's a barn of a place next to an amusement arcade with rowdy slot machines and music playing, but you can always find an empty table and be anonymous there.

'Oh, hi. How are you?' I said, breathlessly. Balancing my coffee cup and saucer, bag and phone I sat down heavily in one of those types of plastic seats that really belong outside.

'Yeah, okay. Where are you?'

He'd rung to tell me he'd slept rough the night before and that his benefit money had not gone into his account as promised. In order to deal with my incoming panic, I finished my coffee quickly, and went to find a bank where I transferred £100 into Will's account, knowing that Guy would not have done so, and probably rightly so. I can't believe this is happening, but if it means he realizes how crazy he is being then maybe being homeless will have been worth it. I think, though, we have a long way to go. I fear for his long-term mental health, which is already in tatters.

Later that day I was sitting in my bedroom looking out at the sea. This is one of the best sea-views I've ever experienced. To one side are the Purbeck Hills, and as the bay curves round to the west as far as the eye can see, the town of Swanage sits confidently. Its lights were just beginning to come on. I was making notes for my next *Diary* entry, wondering how to explain succinctly what had happened that day, then my mind wandered to the future. Picking up my phone, I dialled the *Guardian*'s number in London.

Recently, I had contacted the *Guardian* newspaper to see if they would be interested in running extracts of the online *Diaries* I had been writing for three months by then. They said they would be keen to publish them as a feature for their Saturday Family Section main cover piece. Great! I asked to be put through to the Family Editor, Sally. She said she had nearly finished the editing, and could I give her an update for a brief ending? I told her that I was having a break away from my son, and that William was now homeless. She sounded as if she didn't know quite what to say to this, but we went on to discuss the appropriate wording for the last entry, and she said she hoped the feature would appear within the next two weeks.

19 March

The Diaries *go live*

The *Guardian* piece was published on Saturday, and the website had over 1000 hits (visits), in hours. I have received many hundreds of emails via the website, all asking to be put on our mailing list, and many writing their own stories for inclusion in our 'Experiences' pages. I am so grateful to families for sharing. I believe we can help each other by simply doing just that.

Sally Weale at the *Guardian* did a great job editing the *Diaries*, keeping just the important detail but losing none of the flow. Not an easy task. I am delighted that so many people have found comfort from reading our story. Many of them said how similar their situation was to ours. This has given me a lot of strength. Some of them didn't think we were doing a very good job and I am prepared, of course, to accept constructive criticism. On the whole though, everyone's message was the same – that reading about our experiences has been helpful. I'm really glad, and that is the reason I wanted to be open about what has happened to us.

I was not surprised to read how many of them had had similar experiences to our own family's. My hunch was that there must be very many people who are suffering like us. My aim of setting up the website, and of writing the blog, was to assure others that they were not alone. Many of those emailing have said just that – some of them have quite simply written, 'Thank God I'm not alone'. No, they're not alone, and together we can bring this issue that is affecting our children out into the light to be looked at.

I hope that people will continue to write to me. There is so much power in combined energies, especially passionate ones! I was thrilled that so many people chose to write their own stories down and send them to me. I know that writing really works when it comes to healing yourself. It's very powerful and immediate, but sometimes takes a great deal of courage just to see your own words in black and white on a page. Many of those emailing said that the process of writing their story and sending it to me had made them feel better. I am recommending that they keep writing – send what they write to me or burn it or keep it … it doesn't matter, but keep writing. It will help keep them uncluttered and able to focus better.

Most of us carry around a lot of emotional rubbish that can be cleared out, by putting it down on a page, just as you would empty the bins in your house. Buying yourself a journal, and writing when you feel the need, is a wonderful gift to the self. I know that many times, when my head has felt like it's about to explode, I have sat down for ten minutes to write whatever has come up for me, and I have been able to find my way home again.

I think we should also get in touch with those people who make policy decisions too. I'm suggesting we all write to our MPs and to the Prime Minister. I think that cannabis should be reclassified back again to Class B, to its original classification – that would send out the right message at least. But maybe just raising awareness is enough.

22 March

Moving on

William came to see me the Monday after I returned from Swanage. He phoned first, saying he needed to pick up some clothes. He looked dirty and tired and smelt pretty bad, too. I so often now get a rush of adrenalin when I am with him. I'm still uneasy. My first thoughts are to lock the doors upstairs to protect our property. I've got used to doing this. We need to safeguard things in the house, and I think it's helpful for him too that there isn't the temptation.

'Give us a kiss, then,' I said to him, just like my mum used to do. He bent down to kiss me as he came through the door. I gave him a hug, trying to act as normal as possible, although I didn't know where he had been staying for over a week. I asked him how he was.

'Yeah, okay. How was Swanage?' he asked, looking over at me quite tenderly.

'Good, thanks. Lovely. How have you been? Did you have other clothes with you or…?'

'No, I've been in these same things for 10 days. Haven't changed my pants since then.' He pointed to his underwear.

What? But I'm no longer shocked, more like relieved that he is in one piece. I asked if he wanted a shower. He went upstairs, and I heard him singing in the bathroom like he always does. All his clothes were on the floor outside his bedroom. I took them and put everything in the washing machine, even his coat which smelled strongly of tobacco. There was a yellow form on the bed, which I picked up to read. It was a police caution. I read that Will had been arrested for shoplifting a pair of trousers from a department store in Victoria. It seemed to have happened on the same day that he rang me in Swanage and I transferred money into his account. I replaced the form on the bed, and screamed internally.

We talked later. I made him a sandwich and sat opposite him in the kitchen drinking tea. I asked him what he planned to do, and he said he didn't know. I mentioned the police form I had found.

'Yeah,' he said, smiling. 'I knew I wouldn't get away with it. I was laughing when they caught me. I needed a bed to sleep the night. They questioned me for ten hours.'

Okay, I thought. Not sure what any of this means – a cry for help? He had £100 that day, so maybe. I felt out of my depth. I would have been willing to have Will home again – part of me wants to protect him, and look after him – but Guy is sure that doing that would just lead to a repeat of old patterns. I had rung Guy straight after Will had rung to say he was on his way over. I had begun to talk about options. I talked about Will coming home.

'You're such a loving person,' Guy said, 'but he can't come home. I can't have him upsetting everyone. You'll get stressed when he's back to lying in bed all day and going to bed with the light and telly on. The other boys will get upset. I just can't have that anymore. It's time to think with our minds now, not our hearts. To help him, too. We can set up another B&B place, if that would give you peace of mind. I'm sorry if it feels like I'm giving you orders over the phone – but you do see that he can't live with us any more, don't you?'

I instinctively go into my heart when thinking about my kids, and I know that Guy is right on this one. I'm glad I'm not trying to cope alone; I don't think I'd make a good job of it, especially with sons. I have huge admiration for single parents. One of my difficulties is that I don't yet think of William as a man, yet whenever there is someone of my son's age in the newspaper they are termed 'an 18-year-old man', not a 'boy'. This is something I need to recognize. The upshot of my thinking is that William tries to pull me in, because he must know how easy that is to do – then I get hurt when he lets me down.

Guy has often suggested that I need to look after myself around this issue, and he's right. I guess this must also be a function of the fact I was orphaned and I lived for most of my life with the pain of not having been loved unconditionally by anyone since the age of 12. I never knew my father. He committed suicide when I was two. I grew up believing that my step-father was my 'real' father. It was a relief to find out the lie in this, as he had been rude and unloving to me and my sister for most of our lives. He did provide for us after our mother's death, though, and for that I am very grateful. No blood relatives had stepped forward. It was only when I was 21, and at university, that I found out I had had another father. I remember receiving the death certificate I had sent away for, and reading the cause of his death: 'Multiple injuries consistent with having been hit by a train'. Not trusting anyone enough to share the find, I filed the thing away at the back of a drawer. I instinctively knew that my family would not approve of what I had done, and said nothing. I found out the details about my father years later by getting hold of newspaper cuttings from the time: he had put his head on a railway line and waited for a train to come. He had been a Second World War RAF navigator, and I believe he never got over the fact that he had helped kill thousands in the bombing raids over Germany in which he took part.

My mother became seriously ill, probably from stress, when I was nine, so I had few years of feeling safe and protected. I've always wanted to be a great mother, like my own mum was to me, only over a more extensive period hopefully! I've wanted my kids to have the upbringing I didn't have – a cliché I know, but my lack of love as a child has, of course, informed my parenting.

Jack came home from school quite soon after Will and I had begun talking.

'Hey, how are you, man?' Jack inquired, as he came into the kitchen where we are sitting, looking surprised to see his brother.

While Will was upstairs I asked Jack what he thought about Will coming home, and his eyes flashed as he said it was too early and that his brother needed longer on his own. He told me that *we* needed longer too. He looked anxious that I might decide Will should be with us again. I noted the look in Jack's eyes, and knew that he was right.

The Marios had given me the number of another Italian family who do B&B. I rang them and explained what we needed. Fine, they said. I took Will there and left him. This house was a huge old Victorian place, just off the main drag leading from Lee to Bromley. Most of the houses along the road had been gentrified years before. House prices are steep here. This one looked uncared for, and inside it was dirty and shambolic. A massive weeping Madonna dominated the hallway. She wore a frilly blouse and looked like she needed dusting. *Starsky and Hutch* dubbed in Italian was on the TV, the actors' lips ridiculously out of synch with the dialogue.

We were shown to the vacant room up a flight of gloomy stairs. The walls and woodwork were all painted the same deep brown with a shiny finish. William sat down on the purple nylon-covered single bed; there was a wooden crucifix above it. The landlady was wearing worn red slippers. A short Italian lady in her sixties, she bent towards him waving a plastic-covered set of hand-written rules and began to go through them in alarmingly accented English. Oh, my. I asked if Will could read them later, maybe? It is still amazing to me that Will is not asking to come back to live with us, in a comfortable home in a lovely neighbourhood with loving parents. (The fact even of having parents has got to be a plus. Oh, there I go again.) I recently asked him why he hadn't asked to come back, and he said it was because things never worked out at home with him living there. It seems like I'm the only one who wants him here. Alex is against it too, and gets frustrated with me.

'Why are you so concerned about him? He never thinks about you, except when he wants money. You must admit I'm right, Mum?' he said to me recently, his blue eyes looking directly into mine.

I love that boy so much.

I'm so lucky to have both Jack and Alex in my life.

Two days later the Italian landlady rang me to say she couldn't have Will there any longer. She didn't want someone who is around during the day. I'd been having a tense week, taking Will to see his drugs counsellor, helping him sort out benefit, and trying to get a hold on the anxiety I feel when he is with me. I haven't felt comfortable around him for years. He and I used to be so close, my first beautiful boy who lit up our lives.

We arranged new B&B accommodation for him, or rather I did and Guy paid for it. My husband is really busy at work, which is good because we need the money to support Will. The new address is closer to us, which seems comforting somehow. Less travelling for me too. I got a shock, though, when we arrived at the house, a large Edwardian place on the main road from Lee to Blackheath. This house is next door to the therapist who I have been seeing for some time, more latterly to get support with William. The doorways abut one another, they are so close. This seemed very strange. I'd been next to this front door many times before. I took a breath and rang the jaunty-sounding bell.

The landlady at this new place is a young mother, about 25, a warm, sweet woman who I took to immediately. She was carrying a newborn baby. A little red-headed girl leant against her mother's leg, cocking her head to one side to look up at us. The house was clean and cosy, with no Catholic paraphernalia. Will's room was upstairs at the front of the house. There was a Buddha on the mantelpiece. We seemed to be moving from Catholicism to Buddhism. What's going on here? Everything looked homely. I felt much better about leaving my son here.

Will rang me on the evening of Mothers' Day, Sunday, having heard about the *Guardian* piece from friends. One of his closest friends from school had talked to him about it, he told me. I am friendly with this boy's mother, who works at a national newspaper and who had commissioned the first ever piece I'd written on cannabis. I had told her there was going to be a feature in the *Guardian*, but didn't think of the consequence of her son reading it too, since he no longer lives at home. Damn.

Will began saying how upset he was, and was furious with me for going public with our family's problems. He started crying on the phone, saying that he'd lost everything and everyone. His friend doesn't want to see him, he said.

'I'm trying to move on and you're bringing it all up again. How am I ever going to have a normal life?'

Oh, no. Maybe he has a point? He sounded distraught, and I started to panic, not knowing what to say. Defend myself or ... I could start to feel guilty but pushed that emotion away from me as it came close. No, I know I'm doing the right thing by coming out with the story; I just know it's right. I had already that weekend received hundreds of emails from other deeply sad parents and I felt sure that we could help others. I have repeatedly told William this, particularly at the website's inception, inviting him to get involved and letting him know that his part in this family's story, his 'script' if you like, could potentially be of value to millions around the world. I've talked to him before about the bigger picture and how important he is to it all.

I repeated this on the telephone, then told him to come over, which he did.

He brought me a Mother's Day card. It was beautiful. This was the first card from William I'd had for years. We were all in the kitchen finishing off dinner when he arrived. I asked if he would like anything to eat, and looked over at the virtually empty bowls of potatoes and vegetables on the table. He looked thin, and my heart lurched as I wondered when he had last eaten a hot meal. Oh, God. He sat down slowly and started to cry, saying that he'd lost everything. He shed large tears, which fell on his track-suit bottoms and made a small puddle there. When he was little and used to cry, his forehead would be motley red and his tears profuse. We used to say that we could hold him upside down over the garden to water it. They are the same still.

I held his hand in mine and said that he still has so much in his life. Guy talked about college, and the possibility of getting a job in June when Will finishes his AS levels.

'I think you'll feel better when you're earning money that is yours. It'll give you a lot of self-respect. I know you'll enjoy it too. You've got college still. My advice is to continue there, get your ASs and you can go forwards from there,' he said kindly. 'John is one of your oldest friends; he'll come round, I know he will.'

I talked to him about his drugs counsellor and how he's been getting on with her. Guy asked if Will was still doing cannabis.

'It's the only thing that kills the pain,' he said.

Will was looking down and away from Guy. I squeezed Will's hand

and then noticed the time. It was way past Alex's bedtime. I left Guy and Will and went to shout for Alex. Will left soon after and I heard myself sigh loudly as the door shut behind him. Just how did things get like this? I'm still in disbelief.

28 March

Coming out

The *Daily Mail* has taken up our story and ran a feature based on extracts from the *Cannabis Diaries* last Thursday. There were 2,000 hits on the site within hours of publication, and hundreds of emails and stories have been sent to us. It's such a privilege to read the stories. We have published hundreds now. The response to the publications has been massive. The interest continues. I did an interview for GMTV, the Breakfast Show, yesterday.

Last week in the press and on TV and radio, cannabis was in the spotlight every day, and the message that it is dangerous to children and teenagers seems finally to be getting through. It's interesting how many people will now say: 'Oh, yes, cannabis – it's so much stronger now, isn't it?' where only a few months ago many people would look confused, and blank, when I told them that the cannabis of their youth was not what is being smoked today. Few outside those who were suffering with an addict in their midst, like us, had heard of skunk either. So, things are changing.

I am also delighted that the *Independent on Sunday* has changed its mind regarding legalisation. I think the point we are all trying to make, though, is that it is smoking cannabis in childhood and adolescence that is the prime issue here. (The paper showed some fascinating photos of young brains that had been exposed to cannabis. It was obvious just how fried the frontal lobes are when exposed so young to the drug.) Even if cannabis were legal, we would still have to protect our young people, just as we do with tobacco and alcohol.

I am thrilled that the UN chief, Antonio Costas, has warned Britain about its problem with cannabis. The quote I have put on the home page of our website, from Robert du Pont, rather sums it all up for me: our children are guineas pigs in a ghastly experiment. At no time in history before have young people smoked drugs on a mass scale. The warning is that we should expect to see tragic results; that is what we are seeing now.

I'd now like to set up a lobby group to keep up the momentum about cannabis. I'd like the government to finance properly a health education campaign, just like the one we had for AIDS back in the eighties. It would need to employ powerful marketing techniques behind a zero tolerance approach to smoking cannabis among the young.

Schools need to be supported to get involved in zero tolerance, too. I can't see how they could not be involved. They would be important in ensuring our children are protected from drugs, when out of our care, and in education. My own son started smoking at his secondary school. The approach this school took was that if children were found with drugs they would be expelled, but they did not go looking for the problem. This policy urgently needs extending, with drugs testing in all schools. I believe also that parents and carers are experts in their own right; working together with schools to prevent early drug use among children should be possible.

As to our own family, we are in a better place this week. Guy and I had supper with another couple, two writers, Julie and Jon Myerson, who are going through almost exactly what we are. They came to our house for supper. Jon had emailed me after reading the *Guardian* piece, and we spoke on the phone soon after. He said that he and Julie had been in Southwold, sitting on a bench overlooking the sea, reading the papers that Saturday. Both had looked at each other in silent shock after reading our article. Same profile of child, same dilemmas, same pain. Both he and his wife have written for the *Guardian,* he said. Because many of the details so closely mirrored their experience, some of their friends had suspected that they had written the cannabis feature under an assumed name. I smiled and took it as a compliment.

I think Guy, especially, got a lot out of meeting and talking to them.

I've been lucky enough to have had sessions with my very helpful counsellor, who has worked with addicts, so I've been well supported these past few years. Guy has told virtually no one his personal feelings concerning Will, and for the first time he was given a chance to talk to others who had been suffering in a very similar way. It's very difficult for anyone to understand, unless you've been through it yourself.

Guy was guarded as to what he said at the beginning of our meeting together, but I could see that just speaking about his own pain was helping. He told them that recently he had sat up in bed, startled out of his sleep, convinced at that moment that Will was dead. I looked over at him as he recounted this, not having heard it before and not having been aware of it. Both Guy and Jon agreed that they would trade never seeing their child again, if it meant that they would leave drugs behind, get well and thrive in life.

Guy has always coped with Will's behaviour by getting angry and laying down the firm boundaries that Will has needed in order for us all to survive. Now he seems to be able to move into his heart more easily, which has got to be a good thing for him. Deadening off from our heart's centre always injures ourselves. Keeping the heart open, and the boundaries firmly in place, is one hell of a challenge, but I'm convinced that love can heal anything. You need to be sensible, however, and maintain the love yet also deal very firmly with the addict. There are no clear-cut answers to the problems of living with an addict, but putting yourself and your other children first seems a good place to start. Not getting attached to any specific outcome is something I have had to learn too. Every time I start to hope that we are coming out of the mire, I get disappointed and I am now learning not to do this, because it hurts me. Guy is helping with this, by urging me to protect myself more; I know he is right.

I was alarmed to read in some of the emails that have been sent, that it often happens that the addict begins giving cannabis to the other children in the family. I'm so grateful we don't have that problem. Lots do and that must be very frightening, particularly when the other children look up to the addict and see them as a role-model. Zero tolerance again to drugs in the house is an obvious starting point here, but you have to let them go out...

Will is still living in B&B accommodation, and we are paying for that and putting a small amount in his account every week, for him to buy food. We have offered to pay for him to live in a room in a shared house, until he finishes his AS exams in June. He is in college one day a week, on a Friday, for two separate hour-long sessions with a tutor who comes in especially to teach him. He has managed to get there on time only once.

Last Friday, when I was in the British Museum, about to meet a friend, and have a day off, my mobile rang, and it was Will's tutor asking if I knew where he was. His class started at 9 am. I looked at my watch: 9.40 am. I smiled to myself. If I ever think things may just be improving (or that I'll get a proper day off), you can guarantee that I'm shown that going there in my thinking is not a good idea. I also found out that he had not attended his drugs counselling session last week either, after recently telling us that he was committed to going there every week. I still find it difficult to believe anything he says.

I have found a room Will can rent. We went to see it today; it's about ten minutes from where we live, opposite the huge supermarket in Lewisham. The place is an ex-council maisonette, where the rooms are separately rented out, with a communal kitchen, bathroom and garden. I was annoyed, but not completely surprised, that Will did not meet me at the time we had agreed. I rang him to ask him where he was; he was still in his room. I had arranged to meet the owner, who lives some miles away, outside the supermarket, and he was to show us the property. I had to talk to this man for over ten minutes, silently wondering when Will would show a little more responsibility. This was for him, after all. Though of course, it is also for us. The B&B is very expensive and we need to find somewhere cheaper.

We had a tricky conversation this week. Will had not realized that I was writing an online diary on the website. I think he'd assumed that the *Cannabis Diaries* in the *Guardian* had been a one-off feature I'd written.

'Listen,' he said, when he phoned. 'I love you, right, but could you please stop writing about me. All my friends have been reading what you've written, most of which is lies anyway, and I don't want people to know about everything I do and say. You've got to stop.'

I listened and sympathized, but once again told him about my vision of helping raise awareness of cannabis and if that means telling people about our lives that have been affected so fundamentally, then that is what I will do. I told him again that I was waiting for him to get involved, that he has had a pivotal role in all of this, and that he has a further part to play in helping others – by talking to children about drugs possibly. He didn't want to hear that then, but later mentioned that he too could see that other people could be helped by us speaking out. He seems much more careful, though, about how he behaves around us all. He's been to the house most days. Something has changed. Maybe it's because what he has done, and has become, is not a secret any more, so he has to change even though he didn't want to. I think it's the same with any abusive situation – as soon as other people know about what's going on, the abuser is faced with what they have been doing. It's very powerful, if not nerve-wracking, for the person who is going public with the story.

Will played tennis with Alex yesterday. It was a beautiful spring evening, and they had fun.

I told Guy about this.

'Really? What, he played tennis with Alex? Oh, that's really nice. Do you think he's coming round a bit? He's been to the house a lot too. Oh, but hang on, I mustn't get my hopes up. Every time I do that, I get disappointed.'

I heard a softer tone in Guy's voice, this time, as he spoke about Will. He has felt so hurt and ashamed of his eldest over the years, working so hard and coming home to chaos, often having to write out cheques for large amounts to cover money that Will has stolen or debts that he has run up. He's been so angry. I think speaking to another father who has had similar experiences has helped enormously. Guy has stopped beating himself up about his parenting, and for the first time in years spoke tenderly about his son, without any anger in his voice. The miracles are there to see if you look for them.

7 April

New beginnings

We helped Will move into the shared house last weekend. Just down the hill from where we live in leafy suburbia, there are large areas of council properties that I've never really looked closely at before. The house is set in a development that was probably built in the late seventies, behind an old people's home and opposite a grassed square, with a central cherry tree that is already in full bloom. Although it is just off the main Lewisham to Deptford road, it is quiet there. The house has a small, pretty, garden at the back, the first thing that attracted me to the place. The grass has been recently mown, and the fencing is new. There is a small, perfect camellia bush in full flower and a table, chairs and barbecue are out there too.

The landlord had told me, on the phone, that the other tenants were two young Thai women, and a more mature Polish woman who lives downstairs next to the kitchen, in what would once have been the lounge. He bought the place off the council a few years back as a rental investment. When I rang Will to tell him about the place, initially, and mentioned he'd be sharing with three women, he'd said, 'Well, that's no good. Women hate me! Don't put me off the place before I've even seen it.' I wanted to laugh when he said this. Which women hate him? That's a new one. It could be the girlfriend he stole from, but I guess he's talking about me. I know he feels sore that I'm writing about him.

I had asked the landlord on the phone if the other tenants would have to approve Will before he moved in. He said that wasn't the way things were run, and he was the one who found the new tenants. After he'd shown us around, I wanted to give the landlord a month's deposit there and then; it was cheap, clean – although the kitchen smelt a little of trapped fried food fumes – and on the whole just fine, but Will wasn't happy. As we left the place, he said he'd get mugged every time he went out. I looked around but could only see an elderly man and his plodding dog, slowly making their way down the steps to the main road. But, I'm not a 19-year-old; maybe it would be stressful to live here. So, I shrugged and said if he wanted to try and find somewhere else he could, trying to get the sulky sound out of my voice as I spoke.

We walked over to the supermarket across the road. Will picked up a copy of *Loot* at the entrance, saying he'd look for ads in there and I got a basket, putting a couple of things that I needed in it. As I was queuing to pay, Will asked me if he could get a drink. I said that he could buy it himself; he had money. He took offence at this, and left the store saying he'd see me later. As I watched him leave, with the newspaper in his hand, I realized that he hadn't paid for it.

I didn't have a chance to discuss the place we'd looked at with Guy until the next morning. When I described it, he said it sounded like the sort of accommodation we'd both been living in at university, when we too were 19. Yes, I thought, that's about right. How clever of him to see it that way. I'd been living in a purpose-built flat on campus. Each of the bedrooms was yale-locked and students shared the kitchen and bathroom. Will isn't a student, but seeing things now through Guy's eyes, the house seemed an appropriate place for Will to live.

We were both in the study upstairs. Guy had been looking at his email as I had come in to talk to him. As Guy was speaking I looked over at a newspaper cutting on top of one of my files – its title was 'Lifeclass'. Yes, William 'should' be at university, but isn't, which could be a cause of pain to both of us if we thought about it, which we don't, because that way lies madness. But the message was there for me – he's not a student at uni, but maybe the curriculum, classes and teachers are there all the same, just in a different guise.

Guy said it sounded ideal, and that we should grab it with both hands. I immediately picked up the phone to ask Will how he was getting on with finding somewhere else.

'I've got a couple of numbers, but I haven't rung them yet. I've just been to the gym,' he said.

No sense of urgency, you could say. I felt weak; all this inaction is exhausting. I feel I have my foot gently on the accelerator pedal, trying to help him move forward, but he's slamming his foot on the brake each time. But this is for us too. Rented rooms in shared houses are half the price of bed and breakfast places.

I passed the phone over to Guy, who told Will that we were going to take the room. It was available immediately, and great value, he told him – so could he tell his landlady he'd be moving out by the end of the week? I listened to Guy talking. Good, Will needs to be told like that. I'm so tired, and don't seem able to strike the right note with Will. He seems to drain the life-force from me.

The way Guy sees it, the next step is to get housing benefit in place for Will (he's already receiving Jobseeker's Allowance), so that then we can start to cut ties with him, and hand him over to himself to sort out. Will has been saying that he would get the relevant housing benefit forms to fill in, but still hasn't. I get the feeling that he wants to keep us there for him, to keep the contact in place – a reason to see us.

I rang Will's present landlady, the nice young mum, to check that Will had told her he was moving out. He hadn't told her, she said, and then came an embarrassing moment.

'I saw you on the telly yesterday,' she said. 'I always watch *LK Today* in the mornings, when I'm feeding the baby. I hadn't realized that's what you were going through.'

What? Oh, God. I felt mean not having told her anything about William's history. There was I talking on national television about Will's stealing and appalling behaviour, and I'd calmly left him in her house, saying nothing to her about him. I started gabbling about moving Will out, anything other than to talk about our family. She listened, and said that was fine, then started to talk again about the TV broadcast, which had been a live studio piece about the *Diaries*.

'I understand about cannabis,' she said. 'It breaks families. I should know. Both my brothers are cannabis addicts. They both started smoking when they were teenagers. One of them stole over seven grand off my mum. She's been heartbroken; it's nearly killed her. He's living in a council flat by himself now, and no one in the family wants to talk to him any more. He's in his thirties. He had such a good job, and gave it all away. He can't stick at anything. It's been the same with my other brother too. He's 18 and a complete mess.'

I listened with a sense of unreality as she told me about her family. I'd been reading stories sent to me by email most of the day, and now here was another family story being told to me. I apologized for not having explained more about Will.

'I never ask any questions. It's fine. He's been lovely; no problems at all.'

Well, that was a relief.

Guy and I helped move Will's stuff to the new place. One of the Thai women turned out to be a Thai male instead. He lives in the bedroom next door to Will's room, and came out to welcome Will, in faltering English. He seemed fine; maybe he would dilute the hated female feelings Will had been worried about. Will has signed a lease for six months; as long as he doesn't do anything crazy maybe we can all relax for a while.

I took him to the supermarket across the road (again) to buy groceries. As he pushed the trolley around the shop, I asked him how he felt about his new place. I think I must be programmed always to want my kids to be happy. Here I go again, still anxious after everything Will's done, to ensure he's happy. What is that? If he weren't happy, what would be wrong with that? I've spent a lot of my life being very unhappy, yet I'm still standing. It seems to be important to me – a primary role of mine – to ensure William's happiness, even after everything that's happened. But where is his responsibility in this, though, I began thinking as I asked him how he was feeling.

He smiled and said he was fine.

'It's closer to you too, so I feel it's more controlled,' he said.

He was referring to the time last year when he'd moved away from home. We had offered to pay three months' rent on a place, if he wanted to leave home. He'd hardly been living with us anyway, spending most of his times sleeping on other people's floors. He would turn up when he'd run out of cash, or needed a bath and change of clothes, usually both. He would hardly speak to us; when he did he was verbally abusive. He smelt of that now very familiar odour of weed – sweet yet with unpleasant sour notes. He actually sweated the smell through his pores. He was rude and aggressive to all of us, picking fights with his brothers. Alex was often in tears; a favourite insult of Will's was to tell him he was fat. Jack seemed confused. He loved his older brother, and tried to lighten the ghastly atmosphere by being funny and trying to bring some peace to things, but Will was irritable and moody. I hardly recognized a thing about him.

He had always talked about 'getting us off his back' so he could be independent. When we talked about him getting a job to get his independence started, he said that he would find something himself. We asked him what ideas he had – we often said that maybe he should try the local supermarkets, possibly train to be a manager. He would always yell at us when we made this suggestion, saying that the staff were all retards in supermarkets, and he'd never work there.

We knew that Will was stealing from us, too, although the worst of that was yet to come. He had been kicked out of his school, and was unemployed. There are echoes of that situation again, but Will obviously feels different about things this time.

In January last year, Will had come into some money from a bond invested for him by his grandparents which matured when he was 18. He had received just over £3,000. We thought with that money to fall back on, he could find somewhere away from home to live. We would pay the deposit and first quarter's rent, by which time he would have found a job and he could take over from there. It didn't work out that way at all. His girlfriend of the time said that she thought that one of the reasons Will wanted to live away from us was that he wanted to smoke as much 'draw' as possible, which is exactly what happened.

Within three days, he'd found a flat to live in – over in Streatham, near to where most of his school friends lived. The boy he moved in with had a father who did a lot of cocaine and cannabis, we found out later.

The day he moved out, I felt like he'd died. I left him at his flat, thinking that I hated the place and couldn't understand why William would choose to live in such horrid surroundings when he could be with us. I cried all the way home, wondering if I'd ever get used to the way things had turned out. Guy had been abroad at the time, so I'd done the move by myself. When I got home I went into William's room and sat on the bed, letting myself weep. I started to clean up, and moving the bed to hoover, found around fifty small 'baggies' that had once contained weed. We'd declared the house a drug-free zone years ago, and seeing evidence of the amount of weed he'd been doing helped me stop crying.

That time he left home he never found work, nor did he sign on for benefit. Every time I saw him he seemed dirtier, and stank of weed and tobacco. He gave up cleaning his teeth, it would appear, and one of his front teeth became dark brown in colour. After two months, I talked to him about how he was going to be able to take on the rent of the flat. He told me there was no problem with it, and that he was working in a video shop so he could make the rent.

There was no job. As you will recall, he stole jewellery from my room during his grandmother's eightieth birthday party, which we were hosting, and pawned it. The next month's rent was paid for with a forged cheque of mine he must have taken at the same time. Cheques were also cashed on his girlfriend's mother's account. Chaos.

He came to us in June to say he wanted to come back home. We later found out that he was sleeping on the sofa in his flat – he had given his room to a friend who said he would pay the rent, but didn't. We paid for this along with the outstanding bills and debts that William had built up. It amounted to thousands.

Looking at Will now, I know what he means about things being more controlled. He must have been very frightened too, living in such a mess, feeling completely out of control. He later told a psychiatrist that he always did everything 'to the max'.

I'm feeling that possibly things will be simpler, now he's settled somewhere, but a letter has come from his bank, saying that he is overdrawn. Guy and I are worried by this, but William has said that they are scamming him, and he'll sort it out. I offered to drive him down to the local branch in Blackheath Village. Asking for a printout, the amount he owed appeared to stand at £275. I told him to close the account immediately, and live off cash – that way he can't get into trouble. I withdrew some cash to put into the account to close it, so that we could end this immediately. But Will began to tell the cashier that his account must have been debited by someone else, because the latest transactions weren't his. He had his cash card on him, though, I pointed out.

'This must be someone who knows me,' he said. 'These ATMs on here are all around college – I don't know what's going on here. I did lose my card on that bus, briefly, you remember?'

He reported the fraud, using the bank's phone. I am living in a bad dream from which I just do not seem to be able to wake.

The next day, on the phone, Guy and I talked to him about the fraud. Guy warned him not to take on a bank, because he would never win. Neither of us believes it is a fraud, and now we are fearful that he'll be prosecuted for false allegations, which may mean he'll be unemployable. William stood by what he'd said: someone must have copied his card and used it. I couldn't believe I was hearing this, and started to get very angry with him, saying that the first person they would look to for this is him.

'Don't you think they will find it a bit odd when the card was on you, and the places where money's been drawn from are in the area where you go to school? Not that you've been in for two weeks though, which is another thing that I don't understand. You've always taken out small amounts, too, just like these transactions. It's the same pattern.' I could feel a tight metal band appear from nowhere, wrapping itself around my head.

I calmed down later after sitting in the supermarket underground car park for an hour, trying to get out of the car to buy some groceries, immobilized by anger and upset. I needed to write, the only way to cope here, but nothing to write on. Reaching over to open the glove compartment, I found a notebook I'd forgotten I'd put there. That was lucky. I began to write, and found my way back home to myself, and my heart, which seemed to hold what I needed to get out of the car. It felt like compassion.

As I made my way up the stairs to the store and stepped out into the sunshine, I found myself pushing the 'search' button for William's number on my phone.

He picked up.

'You know I'm really worried about you?' I said.

'You mustn't worry. You get really angry and that's not good, you know. You've no need to worry. You'll see over the next few months, I'll get myself together now. You just have to trust me,' he said.

'I'm worried you're not safe, William. I can't trust you're not going to do something crazy again.'

'Yeah, I know what you mean, but I'm not.'

'I just want you to say grounded, Will.'

'Yeah, that's the word – grounded.Yeah, I need that, that's right. I know.' He was smiling, I could hear it.

I started to tell him that all I've ever wanted was a normal life, how I've never felt the same as other people, never having found anyone who had had the same life experiences. No one I knew had lost both their parents so early on, and could understand how alone I'd felt since I was 12, when my mother died. I had always felt that, because I had never found anyone whose story matched mine, that I must be peculiar, and that it must somehow be my fault, otherwise none of it would have happened. I had wanted a normal life, I continued, and now all this stuff with him had been going on for so long. Will said it all depended on your idea of normal.

'You need to define normality,' he said. 'I've never felt remotely normal, but it's not something I want to talk about on a train.'

Oh, he was on a train. I'd envisaged him in his room.

I began to say that what was happening with the website, how many people had been moved by our story, was not 'normal' either, but was something wonderful, despite its sadness. I don't know whether he caught the last bit because the phone cut off then, but in spite of that it had been a helpful conversation. I felt we'd been able to reconnect on a new level, for a while at least.

14 April

A good week

It's six in the morning; I've been up since five. Guy doesn't sleep well any more. Most nights he wakes at around four, with a scarcely audible sigh, and gets up to read in the study next door, falling asleep again about an hour later. He's been thinking the same early-morning thoughts for years, he tells me – work, money and William, but not always in that order. He's now sleeping again, and I can't.

I've stopped worrying about Will, I've just realized. We've had a better week generally. Things are calmer. Last week, after moving into his new place, he was at our house most days. Generally, he'd ring first to say he needed some more clothes, and then come over and spend time in his old room, mainly using his computer, which is still in there due to lack of space in his new room.

He had come over one morning when I was due to attend an afternoon meeting in London: there has been interest in turning the *Cannabis Diaries* into a book, and I was going up to meet an agent. The Easter holidays had just started, and Jack and Alex were both at home. I suggested to William that he might like to play tennis with Alex again, and left them all in the house together, as I went off to catch a train. I got a phone call about an hour later, just as I was sitting in a Soho coffee shop, drinking latte, and thinking about the impending meeting. It was Will on the phone to say that Jack had thumped him several times, and then thrown both him and Alex out of the house.

'I just wanted to say, that it wasn't me this time. I didn't hit him back, I promise. He pinned me up against the wall. The kitchen carpet has come up. I didn't hit him, though. It wasn't me – just so you know, okay?'

'Is Alex alright?' I sighed into the phone. 'Look after him, won't you? Why don't you both just leave Jack now, and go up to the courts to play tennis? I'm going into the meeting now. I'll phone you later.' I seemed to have stopped breathing.

I spoke to Jack later.

'I can't bear it,' he said. 'He was bossing me about after you'd gone, being really arrogant and cocky. How dare he? He doesn't live here any more and should be acting like a guest when he's here. I told him this, right, and he said that it was more his house than it was mine, pulling that awful face the way he does, so I hit him, and I'm not sorry – he deserved it. Alex started sticking up for him. They ganged up on me, so I threw them both out.'

Fair enough, I thought. It's been a long time coming. I told Jack there was never any excuse for physical violence though, and meant it.

The next day, Guy told me that Will had begun discarding clothes and leaving them on the bed in his room, when he was visiting, before going off again, usually leaving the computer on too. He wasn't happy about this, he said. I remembered the tom-cat spraying he used to do here when he was supposedly living with us, but in reality would only visit once every few days to shower, change his clothes, get more money and then go again, leaving all of us feeling upset and used. Also, I thought that he should have been asking permission to use the internet, in his old room, seeing as he no longer lived with us. But Will's rules of conduct have always been quite different from the rest of us here. And Jack was getting upset with Will being in the house, which needed to be recognized. He's been so wonderful these past few years, not being able to be rebellious due to the fact that Will was doing enough for them both.

Walking into Will's room, I picked up the jeans he'd been wearing when he'd arrived, that were now lying discarded on the bed, along with a hooded sweatshirt I didn't recognize. This wasn't unusual. Since Will had turned 16, and begun living a peripatetic life, most of his clothes and possessions, seemed to be elsewhere and a lot of the time he'd be wearing someone else's things. Frowning now, I picked up the jeans and an empty 'baggy' fell onto the bed. I had hoped never to see one of those things in the house again. I felt a wave of nausea and anger hit me, as the theme tune 'After all we've been through' began striking up its first notes. Nothing makes me more angry than Will bringing drugs into the house ('After all we've been through' now had the added chorus 'and he's still doing it, how dare he?') even though the bag was empty. It was proof he was still smoking too, the idiot. He'd stopped going to his drugs counsellor, and to college – guess that smoking was still his foremost career choice. Christ.

Almost running out of his room and down the stairs, I began rummaging around in the kitchen cupboards. I couldn't find what I was looking for – black bin-liners. Grabbing the back-door keys off their hook on the dresser, I went out to the shed, knowing that there must be garden bags in there. Yes, there were some old ones screwed up in the trug. Good, they would do. It only took me a short time to pack up the rest of Will's things. Guy asked me what I was doing. I knew he'd think that Will wouldn't have enough room for all of his things in such a small room, and logically he was right, but this was for us, not for Will. I showed him the baggy, and the Rizla packet that I'd found under the bed. 'Ah,' he said.

Piling the bags into the car, a voice of my own came in to tell me that of course none of this would fit into his room, that I was going to make a cluttered mess – what did I think I was doing? Getting him out of my hair, I replied. Everything had to go.

Arriving at the shared house, I gave Will the baggy and the Rizlas at the door, and told him never to bring those things into our house again. Guy helped me unload the bags. 'Decide what you want, and I can bag up those things you don't need, and put them in the attic,' I said sharply, feeling better that all of his things were now with him and not with us. Boundaries.

I knew that Jack would feel better too. Guy and I decided that Will should be told that he is not allowed here without either of us being in the house. It's not fair on Jack. His opinion of Will has changed, since last week when he hit him.

We were in his bedroom. Jack was busily hanging up shirts and trousers from the pile of ironing on his bed. Looking around his bedroom, I reflected on how different Jack is from Will. His room is always very tidy; there is never anything thrown on the floor, his clothes are well looked after and always hung up, although there is always a scarily overflowing washing basket. His guitars lean against their amplifiers, and there are electrical cables and professional-looking pedals everywhere. Jack has been playing guitar since he was 12. I'm sure that having that separate dimension to himself has helped him through the difficulties at home with his brother.

'You know the way I always used to stick up for Will?' he began saying. 'Well, I can see what you and Dad mean now. I just looked at him that day, and thought he was so out of order. If I'd been asked to leave, I wouldn't dream of coming back here and throwing my weight around. He should be on his best behaviour. He doesn't live here any more, it's not his house, but as soon as you'd gone he was speaking to me in that way of his. You know how he does. Oh, he's so…ugh. I'm glad I hit him. I don't want to see him. I'm still angry with him. He gets everyone on his side, he draws Alex in. What is it about him? It's the same with Grandma and Martha – they think he's wonderful no matter what he does, like he's a king or something. It's always been the same since we were little. He would get everything he wanted, and still does. Grandma really spoils him, buying him expensive trainers, and giving him hundreds of pounds. Alex and I are not seen as half as good as he is. He charms them, but not me.'

He was referring to Guy's mother and sister, who have both had difficulty in seeing any wrong in Will, looking at us as his family for the answers to Will's behaviour. And Jack is right: Will does have a certain energy about him that is charming and seigneurial. Curious. I feel powerless to help Jack feel any better about all this, just nothing comes to me.

Will rang the next day to apologize about the baggy.

'Sorry about that. I realize that all the good things I have in my life are because of you.' He rather ruined it then, by asking if he was still going to get his money from us as usual this week.

I explained that he would, if he signed on for housing benefit.

He came to the house the next day to say he had done so. Asking for proof before I gave him money, he said that the letters were in his room. It was around 8 o'clock in the evening by this time, and still warm out, so I decided to walk back with him to his house. I'd forgotten how quickly it becomes dark, though, and as we walked down the hill together dusk fell rapidly. I still feel nervous around William, but the 'red alert' feeling has almost gone, so my adrenalin levels are lower. I usually start chatting 19 to the dozen, as my step-dad would have said.

I began telling him about Oz, Jack's guitar teacher to whom I had been speaking that morning on the phone. He'd phoned Jack to tell him he wouldn't be able to come over to teach him that week: his flatmate had hanged himself from the banister at the weekend. Jack had come into my room where I was tidying up, saying Oz was on the phone.

'I think he wants to speak to you, Mum. He's choked up, nearly cry-ing,' he said with the receiver pressed to his shoulder.

Oz told me what had happened, and sounded desperate. He said he just wanted to thank me for helping him the week before. He was talk-ing about the conversation we'd had about women. He had been telling me that his girlfriend had dumped him; this has happened a lot to Oz, who is now in his early forties. This woman had been twenty years younger. I found myself talking to him about what he really wanted from a relationship, telling him that he maybe needed to be really clear about that, really defining what he'd like, even writing down just what he was looking for. Crystal-clear instructions to the universe.

Oz has been coming to teach Jack for two years or so, and is excel-lent. Jack is now really good, and music is a very big part of his life. Guy and I are usually sitting down to supper or to a glass of wine as the lesson finishes, and Oz sometimes joins us. He is a singer-songwriter and in a band, who were recently signed to a well-known label and have a second album out now. He is only a bit younger than us, but lives a very different life.

He wasn't staying for a drink that day, and Guy had yet to return from work, but we chatted in the hallway for a while. I remembered something a woman whom I'd met on a trip to Egypt had told me about attracting love into your life. She'd said that it had really worked for a friend of hers, and I told Oz about this then. He's open to things like this, or seems to be anyway; maybe he simply humours me. But now, on the phone, talking about the trauma of his friend dying so violently in the house they shared, he was saying that what I'd told him last week had really helped, not with finding love it would appear, but with coping with the trauma of the past few days.

That evening some weeks ago whilst we'd been talking, I'd sent Jack upstairs to get a piece of rose quartz and gave the stone to Oz, telling him that in addition to writing down exactly what he wanted in a partner, he should programme the crystal by cleansing it, and then instructing it to help him. He should then light a candle, place the stone and his list next to it and wait for love to enter his life. Simple, apparently!

He looked happy, if not surprised, when Jack dropped the crystal into his hand. I explained what I knew about rose quartz – it was a wonderful crystal for opening the heart and bringing in love. I looked down into Oz's hand and saw that Jack had chosen one of three that I had bought to put in Will's room, next to a picture of himself and me on a beach in Southwold, taken when William was 18 months old. William is looking at the camera smiling, little legs outstretched on the sand, and I am tickling him. I've kept the photo and the crystals in the same place for months now: to bring the love back into our relationship. Not sure if it's working or not, but the crystals are still there, only two of them now; one was off to work somewhere else.

I knew how powerful I had found these crystals were. When I began bereavement counselling, my therapist had advised me to buy one and sleep with it under my pillow. She was careful how she talked to me about this sort of thing, saying, 'I don't want to give you too much mumbo-jumbo.' I'd done as she advised, and know that doing so had really helped kick-start my own healing, to an extent that I would never have believed possible.

Oz talked to me on the phone in a way that certainly touched my heart now.

'I put the candle and the crystal together, like you said. I've kept a candle burning all the time since Joe died, and it's really helped. I just wanted to say thank you. It's funny how sometimes you meet people in life, just by chance, and they really help you.'

It's not me, I wanted to say, I'm just a conduit for these ideas. Instead, I thanked him and told him to buy himself some black tourmaline to dispel negativity. It would help ground him too. I wished he'd been here, so I could give him a piece of mine. Funny how you just want to help, and be there for someone, even someone you don't know very well. It's natural to want to help, I suppose. I told Oz I knew about the effect of suicide, as my own father had died that way. He didn't know, of course, and I didn't go into detail, but maybe the connection helped.

I told Will about my chat with Oz as we walked down to his house, leaving out the mention of crystals and hocus-pocus. Turning into Will's road, I was startled by a man's low whispers somewhere below us. Looking down to where cars were parked below the steps leading up to the housing estate, I saw a man's face appear between the railings. A foreign accent, a wild-looking stare. What the... ?

'Oh, he's some crack-head. Come on,' said Will.

'Have you seen him before, then?' I asked, turning my head to see the man run up the steps towards us. Oh, God, so Will was right about this place, about getting mugged.

The man lurched at us, gabbling something I couldn't catch, but Will calmly opened the front door to his house and we were inside.

'You can't come upstairs. The place is a tip – you'd hate it. You wait here while I find it.' He was talking about the letter confirming he'd applied for housing benefit.

Moving into the kitchen I could just make out the man through the net curtains. He was dancing, his arms held high, and moaning loudly. I could see him picking up a long metal pole, and waving it about. Oh, my God, I'm leaving my son here. This is awful. There was a sign by the cooker, in poor English, asking everyone to clean up after use. (I guessed it was written by the more mature Polish lady who lived in the lounge bedroom.) Some hope with my son, but good luck with that.

Will came down again to say he couldn't find any proof about the benefit. Guy and I had decided that we would tie in getting an allowance from us with him making the effort to apply for his rent to be paid, so that we wouldn't be in the same situation as last year, when we paid hundreds of pounds in rent owing, and other debts outstanding. It had to be different this time.

'Ok,' I said, not believing he'd applied and now here was the confirmation. 'I can't give you any money, then, until that's done, but if you like I can pay for some groceries.'

'Yeah, okay. You can't walk out of here by yourself anyway,' he said.

So, he was going to make sure I was safe from that marauder. But were we both safe, even together? It's at times like these that I realize how protected I've been living where I do. Later, when I saw the police arresting the man on the main road, I wondered why I hadn't called the police myself, as if I believed that living 'down here' meant that you were prey to people like him, and you had to put up with it. Where did I pick up that idea from?

We walked out of Will's house and made our way down the steps. The man came bouncing over to us, telling us in, faltering English, that he was Czech and had been arrested for stealing something from a shop and now couldn't get a job. Stealing, eh? Well, that's something we know about. He'd ditched the pole. Will was very calm and spoke to him gently, saying that we couldn't give him anything, and that he should leave us alone.

Phew. We made it over the road to the supermarket, and went in. I thanked William for being so calm and helpful.

'That's okay, Mum.'

The next day Will dropped round with the confirmation that housing benefit had been applied for. He said he'd been up early and gone to the Jobcentre, and then onto Charlton and Millwall football clubs to ask about work and training projects that they might be running.

'I've had a really good day. I've found a free course starting in two weeks; it may lead to getting a qualification to do football training. There was a guy at Millwall who said it would be just the right thing for me; he told me to apply to the press office too. I told him how I had thought about being a sports journalist and he said to apply.'

We both sat down at the kitchen table and he passed me the leaflet about the course.

A shaft of sunlight suddenly entered through the window, like someone had just switched on a spotlight outside to illuminate the space between us. Slow-moving silver particles, trapped within the narrow beam, caught my startled gaze as they began a slow, whirling dance.

'I know you probably won't approve but... ,' Will began.

Wouldn't approve? He was talking about the course he had decided on, which the leaflet advertized. I said well done, and got up to lean across the table to give him an enthusiastic hug. He has done all this by himself.

I reminded myself that if you try to help a butterfly out of its cocoon, it dies, because it has to do it for itself. Without the personal, often painful effort, it doesn't have the strength for life. Maybe this particular butterfly is now ready to emerge from its cocoon.

The beam of light went without my noticing. How did I miss that? I looked over at William, and was struck again by how beautiful his eyes are – light, yet bright, blue. It's his eyes that are the first thing to give it away when he's 'blazing', and I can tell that today there is a change. A good day.

26 April

Going home

A great many people have written to me in response to the interview that was published in the *Sunday Times* at the weekend, linked to the conference at Wellington College where I was speaking about our story and the website. In the paper there was a photo of me holding a puppy. In between going to conferences, and having a birthday, I have been on hands and knees scrubbing carpets and going in and out of the garden with a new member of our family. Her name is Lily, and she is an eight-week old blue roan cocker spaniel.

The idea of a dog came to me when I was in Swanage. I noticed, as if for the first time, the large numbers of wellie-wearing dog-walkers on the beach in the early morning, most of whom carried in one hand long curved plastic things that seemed to have a bit on the end to grip a tennis ball. Looking down from my hotel bedroom, I watched as unleashed dogs trotted beside their owners, or zig-zagged around sniffing at the sand and flirting with the sea. Looking closer, some of them seemed to be almost grinning. The dogs I mean. They seemed to be everywhere I looked. It reminded me of when I bought my first car, a VW Beetle; I seemed to see hundreds of the same car everywhere after that when I had hardly been aware of them before.

Walking on the beach at Swanage that week, with myriads of dogs leaping out at me everywhere, a black stone in the sand caught eye, and I bent down to put it in my pocket. As you know, I have an interest in crystals, and I'm willing to believe that stones from the sea may also have helpful properties, and let's face it I need all the help I can get right now!

Once back in London, I placed it on top of a small bookcase in our kitchen, not really asking myself why apart from the fact that it would remind me of my holiday. A friend who runs her own crystal importation company was at my house soon after. She had come over to see our new puppy. Picking up the stone to ask me about it, and turning it over and over, she said how similar its markings were to a little puppy pawprint. 'What?' I asked, and taking the stone from her, looked at it afresh and saw that she was right.

'Clever little Lily, she bi-located to be with you,' said my friend, who seemed to know about things I was only vaguely conscious of. Bi-what?

After she had gone I chanced to look up at our kitchen noticeboard to see a request I'd written out, dated, and pinned up there. October last year was the date. That was when we were in the middle of excluding our eldest son – again. I remembered that I had read a review of a new book about the concept of a 'cosmic ordering service'. It seemed that you simply ask in a very straightforward manner for what you want, and you should receive it. Inspired by this idea, I had asked simply for 'peace for the whole family' (please!). A desperate plea I'd sent out and then forgotten about.

Doing some quick calculations, I realised that Lily would have been conceived the month I'd penned my 'order' and been born the week before I'd gone to Swanage. Magic – or just good timing? It doesn't matter, and maybe they are one and the same thing anyway. But the idea of a dog had never occurred to me until that week in Swanage.

Returning home, I asked Alex what he thought about our getting a spaniel puppy. It had to be a female blue roan spaniel, that was my only stipulation. We had looked after a friend's spaniel, Hattie, for some years during the summer holidays until she was tragically run over whilst on a walk with her owner. We had all loved that dog.

Alex was off school unwell, and lying in bed. He sat up saying he knew about dogs, he'd been reading about what you need to do to look after a puppy on the internet recently. (He had?) The look on his face was all I needed to know. I had found the key to something. We looked on the Kennel Club website. Details of six blue roan puppies had been added to the list of puppies for sale that day, and one of them became ours – Lily, Lady of Lydden.

Never having owned a dog before, I was nervous about being a puppy-mum, but she has brought into the house what I had hoped she might – a lot of fun and distraction. The boys love her, and when Will has been to the house, Lily has made a fuss of him too.

It's been like having a new baby, though, and has brought back memories of those first days when I was alone with William, after everyone had gone back to their normal lives, and I was left with what seemed, at times, like the overwhelming responsibility of making sure a new young life was safe in my hands.

There has been a lot going on here, just for a change! Alex was mugged last week, on my birthday, as he made his way back home from the bus-stop. He had been mauled and pulled about by three older boys he'd never seen before – they tried to get his ipod and phone out of his blazer pockets. One of them threatened to punch him, and Alex handed both items over. He is now seeing the school counsellor, and has mentioned what he has been through with William too. He says it's helping him.

Yesterday we received a letter from Will's college in Kensington, saying that they had made the regrettable decision not to have him back this coming term. They had wanted to exclude him in January, and maybe they were right then to believe that it was hopeless. As you'll recall, Guy and I pushed for him to be allowed to continue with his AS courses, to get those qualifications at least, of which he has done half up to now. It seems sad that he was close to finishing them, but there was a mock History exam last Friday, to which he did not turn up, apparently.

Will is still saying that he did go in for it, but the college says he didn't, and in their letter add also that he has only turned up for four out of a possible 12 sessions since January. They have had enough, and who can blame them? It worries me that Will is saying he did sit the exam; he sounds genuine. This is often the case – he says one thing, others say another – you enter through a portal into a land where nothing is certain, and, when you try to get to the truth, it's an almost impossibly perilous journey.

On Monday, he began the short football coaching course that we had talked about, or so I believe and hope. He rang me last night, though, to say he was ill and hadn't been that day. He sounded awful, very blocked up and weak. He then went on to say that he knew now that he needed to quit cannabis.

'I know I've said this before when I was in the Priory, but I need to quit. It's ruining my life. I know I'm ill now, but I've been thinking and all I know is that I'm stuck in this little room with no future. I've got nothing and it's got to change. The course is the only good thing in my life.'

I had just that afternoon been speaking to someone from Marijuana Anonymous (MA) UK, who rang me in response to an email I'd sent via their website. I'd been interested in what meetings there were in this country, and a young woman from London contacted me. I was mainly interested to know because 'Talking about Cannabis' is setting up support groups for parents and carers, and I wanted to find out what resources there might be out there, in the form of groups for users. As she spoke, though, I began to think that the meetings she described might be helpful to William. Now he was talking about quitting, I told Will about the groups – all of which are in London. He listened and said that he'd think about it, sounding very far away, but then mentioned Sally, his drugs counsellor, saying he should ring her.

We had had a difficult time after the Easter weekend: Will had been at our house most days, which was fine, although every time he came over we all did a pincer movement, locking doors upstairs, putting valuables in the safe again, making sure there were no temptations around for him. Exhausting but necessary. But later that week, we realized that a couple of things had gone missing from the house. Jack had lost a new (expensive) sweatshirt, and Guy's mobile phone couldn't be found. On the following Wednesday, Guy and I had been out and returned to find Will in his favourite position, sitting at the piano in the front room.

'Oh, hi,' I said, trying to sound friendly, but struggling. 'How are you?'

'I didn't ring 'cos I've lost my phone,' he said.

I've lost count of the number of phones he's had and lost. This one I know he has had only briefly, a couple of months maybe.

'Yeah, I lost it on a bus. It must have fallen out of these trousers. That was how I lost my wallet too.'

'So, what does that tell you about putting things in those pockets, then?' I said, trying to keep calm, and not sound like Joyce Grenfell talking to a four-year-old.

'Yeah, I know, I'm a retard.'

Oh, crumbs I wasn't expecting that. So what do I say to that except 'you're not', which I managed to come up with, of course?

'William, you know that Guy has lost his phone?' I said nervously. Will was still sitting on the piano stool in his coat. I was talking to him from the hallway.

'I've got it here. That's why I came over. I went to see Sally and she said to come home and give it back and things would be fine.'

Oh, right.

'Well, good that you brought it back. That's good. I'm pleased.'

Guy wasn't and asked him to leave.

'Even when you're not living here, you're stealing from us.'

He said quite a lot more too, and began going red from anger.

I found it impossible not to go after William. We sat in the car and talked. When I asked him about Jack's sweatshirt, he said he didn't take it. He went on to say that he was just a failure and didn't know why he'd taken the phone. He'd been back to the house since he took it and didn't return it then and couldn't understand why.

At times like these I always talk about drugs and how he's got to quit. The woman from MA told me yesterday that they talk very little about drugs, but a lot about recovery, which has given me much to think about.

Now, he's been kicked out of another college and is ill. Possibly the 'rock bottom' everyone talks about? I don't know. I do know that I'm very tired of this roller-coaster and just wish William could take the help that is there for him, and turn his life around. But, of course, it's not that easy for him, as he always tells me.

We sat in the car and he began saying that everyone hates him and rightly so, and cannabis was his painkiller, the thing that did it for him.

Not alcohol, like a lot of people, he said, but cannabis. When I asked him what he needed to make things better he said that someone older to take him under their wing would be good. Like a mentor? I asked, trying to think of someone, but coming up with noone. Why couldn't I think of anyone? But I couldn't.

I'm trying not to build hope that he may now get better. Addiction is so confusing. We saw one another again this morning; I took him to a local café near his house for breakfast; I was having to make a conscious effort not to hold my breath out of nervousness. What's the matter with me? Christ, get a grip – this is my own son. I could feel the headache that I have almost permanently at the moment begin its familiar beat. I told him that one of my friends had read the last diary entry and rang last night to advise me not to make any further mention of crystals again, in case people think I'm a 'crackpot', as she put it. It's got me thinking about 'self-censorship' as she called it. I asked William what he thought, and he grinned, saying that most of the mothers that he'd ever known round here were crackpots. He went on to say that when he'd been lying in his room feeling awful, he'd been thinking about how much I'd taught him over the years about how to look after himself.

'Do you think the mind can make you ill, would you say? Is it just a state of mind?' he asked, rubbing his forehead.

We talked, and I wished I could be more relaxed and enjoy our times together more. I want to repair the damage, but don't dare to hope that it can be done. It really is a matter of trying to appreciate the moments of peace that we have together. When we'd finished eating, William said he was still feeling ill and asked if we could go and buy some 'rescue remedy'. It was my turn to grin then. We went to the chemist, and I bought him Day Nurse and vitamins instead, which I knew would help him more. I drove him back to his house and he seemed better. He'd said he'd needed to get back in touch with us, to go home, and when we're wobbling perhaps that's what all of us need – we all need a concept of 'home', wherever or whatever that might be.

9 May

Making the changes

It's been an active couple of weeks. The initial meeting of the Talking About Cannabis Action Group took place in London on Friday, and in the two weeks leading up to it I was very busy making preparations. But we are now launched, all of us in the steering group are determined to push for the investment in a 'massive health education campaign' that was promised but has never materialized. We are in the middle of a cannabis epidemic and everyone needs to take it seriously. We also need to be teaching children from an early age about the dangers of the stuff, and we as a group are going to look at the most effective way of doing this.

Education about cannabis is central to the whole issue. The knock-on effect of young people taking this so-called 'soft' drug on health and on crime must be obvious to everyone, but not enough people are taking the problem seriously. That needs to change. Young people are the future of every society, and need protecting. They are often not in a position of sufficient maturity to make their own decisions about drugs; they need to be guided by sensible adults so that they can reach adulthood in good mental health.

Sadly, this is not the case for William. He has just rung me saying he is walking around the streets with nowhere to go. He has left the football course he was doing, and I begin to wonder whether he ever went along at all. Knowing what is a lie and what is the truth is one of the most challenging things about William.

When I got back from the meeting on Friday, tired and slightly concerned about Lily, our new puppy, who had been on her own for a couple of hours, William rang at the door. What I really wanted to do was to kick off my shoes and sit down with a cup of tea, but it seemed that that wasn't what was planned for me. Wonder why I let others take the lead so easily and fit in with them? I have some answers – the skill of fitting in with others was central to survival after my mother died. I became adept at reading other people – anticipating their moods and their needs. Keeping others happy at the expense of my own needs became essential for my continued existence, although a bigger part of me would have liked to have tossed the whole board game and pieces up into the air and gone with my mother. I couldn't believe she had left without me, leaving me with – well, who was going to look after me now?

In the ten minutes since I'd been in, I had already noticed that Will had obviously been in the house that morning, whilst I was out. Jack must have let him in. I knew he'd been there because a stick of his concealer make-up was left open in the bathroom, and the computer in his room was on. My first thought was that my jewellery had not been locked away – oh, no. But my bedroom door was fast. Jack must have had the presence of mind to lock it when his brother arrived. Unfortunately, he had taken the key with him, so I couldn't get in there.

Placing my handbag over my arm, I would now have to take it round with me; usually I lock it in my bedroom. I started to chat to Will – how was he, how was the course going? I asked him if he wanted to sit in the garden. It was a sunny day. Breathing deeply, I put the kettle on and made a cup of tea – my friend in everything. I'm drinking too much caffeine and not eating properly (my voluble inner critic starts to message me). Opening the cupboard I took out the McVitie's chocolate biscuits – delighted there were any left. The link with my mum again; I began to catch myself wishing she was here.

It was very warm, and the garden was looking good in the sunshine. As we sat down I could feel a heaviness start up in my neck, and tried to relax. Will began talking about how he needs to give up cannabis. He was looking relaxed, his eyes were clear – always a sign that he is off the weed. Last week he'd come over to the house saying that he had been feeling desperately ill; he had had a virus of some kind. He'd told us that while he was lying in bed with noone to look after him, he'd realized a lot about his drug dependency and knew he needed to quit cannabis. I began talking about the drugs counsellor, encouraging him to go back to her, and I also mentioned again the Marijuana Anon meetings that I'd thought sounded appropriate.

'So, when are you going to help me with the website and get involved with helping other people, then?' I began saying.

'Yeah, well, yeah. Of course, yeah, I'd like to. Think I could be good at that too. You need to get them young, though. All this talk of drug-testing in secondary schools – you'd have nobody left over the age of 13.'

We both laughed, although I knew he was being serious too.

We talked about the possibility of us putting workshops and presentations together for schools, and I looked at Will at that moment and hoped that we were on a new pathway, possibly together, something I had always believed would happen. It was just a matter of when.

One of the people who had been at the meeting that morning, Carla, who is a drugs counsellor and workshop leader, had asked me and another mother who was there, if our sons would like to earn some money by giving talks to children on their experiences of cannabis addiction. I told Will about this; we had already talked the week before about the possibility of this happening – I'd been so pleased that he might be able to work with me. Now here was another opportunity to get involved. Will immediately called Carla.

I smiled to myself, and wondered if there might be a happy ending to the *Cannabis Diaries* after all, or indeed whether I might soon have nothing to write. Guy had said to me after Will had gone following last week's visit that he was glad I'd decided to write the *Diaries*.

'Maybe it's a matter of "if you can't beat them, join them" for him now,' he said, smiling.

We both laughed.

'Dare we think this time, that he means it, do you think?'

I told Will what his father had said and he smiled, saying that that was pretty accurate, and that he hoped I'd stop writing altogether. I know it's been hard for him to have his story published on the net, but

I also recognize that he has chosen to modify his behaviour; that much is obvious, knowing that I may write about it in the next few days. It's the only control we've had for a long time! I've also always said that it is his gift to write the end of the story.

We talked for an hour or so, with Lily playing around us, and I began to feel tired and wished he would go so I could get some time alone. He seemed to be reluctant to leave and I asked him if his claim for housing benefit had been processed and if he had received any notification.

'Yeah, well, that's a problem and my landlord is at the house at the moment saying that I need to pay him his money. I've given him half of this week and now I have nothing left.'

So, he needed money. But we had had a sensible conversation and he'd been well behaved and seemed to be drug-free. I also needed him to go now; my eyes were closing as the emotional tiredness kicked in. So, I suggested that I pay his rent for another two weeks, up until the end of next week, so that we don't alienate the landlord, which is a pattern with Will. We really don't want to be having to find him somewhere else to live. His new place is cheap and close by (an advantage for who I'm wondering now). Most of the times that Will comes to the house it's when he doesn't have money, but our relationship with him has been that way for many years. But with him living elsewhere, I feel I can cope a lot better.

I wrote out a cheque payable to the landlord. He asked me if I can sub him with some cash until he gets his giro next week. He told me that he hadn't been able to sign on, due to doing the football course, so his giro would be late. I sighed, and told him that signing on had got to be a priority – why are things that are so obvious to everyone else so difficult for him to understand? Then I remembered the research about the mental processing difficulties that go with skunk addiction that I'd been reading. There is the problem of only looking at short-term gain, the inability to plan even for a few days ahead, or to construct goals for the future, and the lack of ability to learn from mistakes that keeps addicts repeating the same nightmarish patterns. There is also the issue of getting cash for drugs; once that's gained other planning just doesn't happen.

We didn't see Will again over the Bank Holiday – another pattern: once he has money we don't see him again until he's run out.

He came over yesterday and I asked him if he had run out of cash.

'You always think I'm here only for money, don't you? What the hell sort of parenting is that?'

'Will, I'm asking you because often that is the case.'

He took a piece of paper from his pocket. I've seen one of these before – a whole bunch of them last week on Friday when he came over to see me after the campaign group meeting. They are print-outs of available jobs from the Jobcentre. I began to wonder if he thinks these bits of paper placed on the kitchen table are the passports to me shelling out cash.

'I'm going for this bar job. I've got an interview but I need money to get there. I can't do the course any more 'cos I need to find a job,' he said.

When Guy came in he told Will that he was not going to sub him any more money.

'You need to sign on in time. Every time there's been a problem with you getting your benefit. It always seems to be late because you don't get there on time. You need to sort the housing benefit too; we can't afford to keep bailing you out. It's not good for you either. I don't mind buying you food, but I'm not going to give you any more cash.'

Will went back to his house after that.

He's not happy about what his father said, and returned this morning to plead with me. I asked him to leave. I don't like feeling besieged in my own home and I'm on the verge of asking him not to come over uninvited.

He rang me this afternoon to say he had nowhere to go, and no money, no credit for his phone, the list went on. I listened, but didn't invite him over. It's confusing because last night whilst he was here I asked him if he wanted to write something for the website, and he sat down and wrote his current view of cannabis, which is a negative one, and included his plans to quit. I almost wonder now whether he was doing this so that I would agree to give him money. Today, Wednesday, is the day he normally goes up to college to play football with the team, and I know he went last week even though he'd been expelled, which seemed odd. So, maybe he was hoping to go again today, hence the story about going for an interview. I wouldn't be surprised – it's happened many times before.

You never know, though, when someone is going to begin making the changes that they talk about. I'm delighted that he wrote the piece for the website; that in itself will have concretized, even if only for that moment, what is in his thoughts and that action by itself can be the precursor to change.

22 May

I used to care, but things have changed

Alex is in plaster. He broke his foot whilst doing athletics at school last week. This is the second time in six months, though last time it was the opposite foot, so I suppose there is some sort of balance to it. But, he's frustrated and unhappy. Like most children he loves sport, and is feeling upset that he won't be able to take part for many weeks to come. Guy is furious with the school; neither of us feels that enough care has been taken for our child to have broken bones twice whilst in their charge. I think, too, that Guy is angry that just as we remove one strain from our lives – having Will no longer living here – Alex needs extra attention.

I am concerned that Alex is suffering. You may remember he was mugged in April; then he had a discus dropped on his foot two weeks later. He has been seeing the school counsellor to help him over the mugging. He says that he is looking around him now as he walks along the street, to see who might be about to pounce. I remember when Jack was mugged whilst waiting for a friend on a railway station; he was hit around the face and threatened. He was about the same age – 13. Jack was nervous for a long time, and saw a counsellor too. When we walked together he would often be looking for me out of the corner of his eye, just to make sure I was still there. Now it's happening again with our youngest.

Alex first asked if he could have counselling back in January this year. 'So I can let it all out about Will. I've got a lot to say. I think it would be good for me.'

I asked at our local surgery, but no appointment came. After chasing it up twice, I gave up. I'm not sure why I go to that GP practice; I think it's because I don't have the time to change, but probably should.

Alex has been talking to the school counsellor about the mugging but also about Will, and the counsellor has told him that the mugging has re-opened old wounds – he was stolen from by his brother and now stolen from by strangers. They have also discussed the fact that he feels he needs to be good at home, so he doesn't add to our stress, and that he sees his role as that of helping smooth things over.

We were standing in the kitchen when he told me this. I was about to put the kettle on so we could have a cuppa together. I put my arms around him and apologized, saying that he doesn't always have to be good and if he wants to be naughty to go ahead. Alex grinned then, and gave me a kiss.

'It's okay, Mum. I don't want to be.'

But he seemed sad, then.

'You know that talking about things can make you feel worse at first, but later you do feel better. It's not always immediate though,' I said, looking anxiously at him.

He said he understood, and began chatting about how I'd like his counsellor – and maybe I knew her? Greta van de Something. No, I said, I didn't.

'Well, you know I told her you'd been writing about our family and she said, "Not Debra Bell – is that your mum? I've read some of her *Diaries* in the paper." I said, "Yes, it was" – so how about that, Mum? She'd heard of you. I was really proud!'

We both smiled, and I was amazed that this woman had heard of me. She would have known more about Alex than Alex had told her, too, if she'd read the *Diaries*, which might mean that she could leap-frog a little when talking to him.

It's funny because when Guy and I were discussing whether Will should be asked to leave the house last time, Guy talked about the effects of the family's situation on the other boys. He's always talked like this, saying we have to protect them.

'You know what it was like for you in your childhood, living with trauma, and how you say it affected you. I remember you saying how you used to hide away, but you could hear your stepfather beating your sister and how awful that was, how it's stayed with you. You have to be careful with kids.'

I knew he was right, but it wasn't something I was particularly focused on, because I could see how loved our kids were and how much abundance was in their lives. Guy was right, of course – just because kids were from privileged backgrounds didn't mean they couldn't be damaged.

'Look at it this way. If social services looked at our family and saw how our 19-year-old steals from our 13-year-old and causes such heartache for the whole family, they could choose to remove him from us. Alex has asked for counselling, for Christ's sake! That has upset me more than anything – our 13-year-old needs to see a counsellor. What exactly are we doing here?'

I knew he was right, and this made our decision to exclude Will much easier for me.

There is also something in my life now which has helped me deal with Will in a much firmer way – creating even clearer boundaries, which must be good for Will as much as for myself. I knew that getting Lily would be beneficial – but was unsure as to how. I can see now that drug addicts and dogs are not dissimilar. They both want instant gratification, and then they are on to the next thing.

If I let her, Lily, who is just three months old, would use this house as her playground. I am learning to give commands and expect her to obey. 'Sit' and 'No' are needed to create firm boundaries, otherwise you have chaos. You still love them madly, but it's all very clear who is in charge. This is all so new to me. I think it's something we've lost in modern parenting – either because parents are working, so therefore feel guilty and give and give in too much, or whether, like myself, they just feel they want to be very loving, child-centred parents and to take their cue from the children. This inclination was backed up by the books I read when they were younger about child rearing. I think we need more of this black and white clarity when dealing with our kids.

Now, with Will, I find it easier to say 'No', and then possibly negotiate (or not). Before I would always say 'Yes', and then negotiate, which meant I was in a weaker position, and it was exhausting too trying to backtrack and feeling guilty and confused. I needed to learn to let Will sort out his own problems – my taking them on for him doesn't help anyone. It is more clear-cut with him anyway, now. He is no longer at college, nor on any course, nor does he live with us. We have told him that any requests for money need to be made through his father, and that we will buy him food and clothes if he needs, but we will give him no more cash.

Last time he came to the house he told me, as he was leaving and we were standing in the front garden watching Lily leaping into the bushes, that he needed money, and I repeated that he needed to talk to his father about that. He then said that he had a cheque from the DSS but nowhere to pay it in as his bank account was closed. I presumed he meant that there was still an ongoing check on the fraud he'd reported whilst I had been with him in the bank last month.

I told him to open a savings account, but he said that he had a zero credit rating so couldn't. He went then, leaving me wondering whether he would ever simplify his life. Calling for Lily to come in, I closed the front door and then noticed a letter on the table in the living room. It was one of Will's that he had just opened. Irritated with the way he leaves things here still, I picked it up and read that it was a demand from his bank to pay off the amount he owes, which is now nearly £300 with interest accruing constantly. No mention of an enquiry into the fraud he was maintaining was made against his account. So there had been no 'scam' as he had put it. Good of them not to prosecute him, I suppose.

He had called an hour later to say he had locked himself out of his room. I said I'd bring him a ladder to help him get through his open bedroom window, and I took the letter with me.

Jack had just returned from school. He helped me put a ladder in the boot of the car, and we drove down to Will's place together. I came over all puppy-mum-like when I saw him. I thrust the bank's letter into his hand and told him to sort it.

'You have a cheque, you say. You need to pay it into this account and clear the amount owing. You're still using our home address as your own; this could affect our own credit rating, so if you don't do it for yourself, do it for us. I'm this close to cutting you off completely – so get it sorted.' I motioned with my thumb and my first finger as I said this, then turned and got into my car and drove away.

He rang later to say he'd deposited the cheque in his bank and had made an arrangement to pay off the debt. I told him I was glad he'd done this and taken responsibility, but silently wondered how he is going to do that when he was on benefit only and has no other income. No mention from him of that day when I stood by him as he made the call to the fraud department, to report a theft on his account. I haven't mentioned it either.

He rang the next day, crying, saying he had no money and did I know what that was like for him. I took him some Tesco vouchers that had just arrived – £24 worth – so he could eat at least.

He rang over the weekend to say he'd been attacked by 20 people at a party in Notting Hill, and beaten up. I saw him yesterday and he had a black eye, which was just discernible. I asked him what they took.

'Nothing. There was nothing to take,' he said looking down at the mobile phone in his hand. Oh, that's right, you have no money, I thought.

I don't know how to talk to him any more. Most things he says are lies, so how can I have a relationship with him? It silences me. Curious. Jack says that Lily is a symbol that we are moving on as a family, and sends out clear messages to Will. One thing is obvious – she has brought us all closer together and even Guy (who jokes to friends that he 'fought a valiant rear-guard action against having a dog') has to admit that she's very beautiful. People stop us a lot to smile and say how gorgeous she is. She has brought a lot of joy to us, and to others too. We begin dog-training lessons this morning. Moving on.

5 June

How to save your own life

I've been dropped by my agent; it was nice while it lasted. She wasn't sure she could guide me as to how the *Cannabis Diaries* should look as a book. Okay. Over the past three years I've written two books which I know are urgently needed in the world, and they sit there looking at me from out of their file covers, waiting to be published. Then there are these *Diaries*, which may or may not constitute a book, but what seems to have happened is that I now I seem to be 'just' writing for the website and 'just' setting up an Action Group. I say 'just' because I find I have so little time for anything else right now.

My vision for myself was not this, but I'm prepared to trust that I'm on the right pathway, needing merely to adjust my lenses to allow myself to view this new life that seems to have appeared, one where we have lost one of our kids. We did what? When I allow myself to think about what has happened to our family, I get this pain deep in the centre of my stomach. How did it get like this? No answers, though; only questions which colour the air in front of me as I verbalize them, making me more aware each time that I'm doing work that is urgently needed. I'm convinced that we can help stop the next generation of children from becoming dope smokers, and put an end to the resulting trauma and misery that affect families.

I know that Guy, too, is confused and disappointed with the way life has turned out. He said last week that he was grieving for the family he once had. We were sitting in the kitchen having breakfast as he began speaking, both of us looking out at the Bank Holiday rain. He sighed, saying that when he sees William he feels intense irritation, and doesn't know how to communicate with him, because of the endless lies, but when he's not in contact with him he's worried about him. It's almost as though, he said, looking down at Lily, that we've replaced William with a puppy.

Before Lily arrived we all made jokes about how we could put her in Will's old room, and send her to his old school, where Alex goes now. We were laughing and saying that it wouldn't be possible because it is a boys' school. Yeah, right, not the only problem with the plan, Jack said.

Alex played with Lily when he got back from school yesterday, and put his school tie around her neck. She was running around with that on for a while until Guy, with a frown, told him to take it off her – maybe he was reminded of that conversation then; I know I was.

As I said before, having a puppy has helped us all, including William by default. She is hard work, although I spend less time on hands and knees cleaning now. It's much easier when the sun is shining and I can open the back door to let her out and in. It must be obvious to Will that we are moving on with our lives, without him, and getting attention from us is more difficult now. Last week he rang me, sounding on the verge of rage as he began asking how I was. I knew he was feeling sidelined and ignored, and he said as much.

'You don't ring me any more. What sort of a mother are you? I got beaten up last weekend, and you just didn't seem to care. How am I supposed to cope on my own? I'm a teenager. I can't do it alone. I don't know what to do. I know I've made mistakes, but you're up there in your big house looking down on me – casting me aside as if I was a piece of dirt you could throw to one side. You've got to admit it was your parenting that landed me here. I know I'm to blame too, but it's 60:40 here, you must admit.'

I wasn't sure which amount of the equation was supposed to be mine – the 60 or the 40. I told him that I'd lived alone in the past; I knew how difficult it was and that was with no family at all.

'Yeah, well, what's the difference then – apart from choice? I have no family, and I'm on my own.'

'You do have a choice,' I said. 'You chose to abuse your family, and we're not going to let you do that, so now you have to work things out on your own. I can't believe anything you say. We're getting on with our lives. I have two other children to think about, so you're going to have to move on too. Don't come to the house uninvited, do you hear me? I've told you this before and you still turn up – that is not allowed – do you understand?'

William had come to the house the day before, when Alex was here alone and Guy and I were out. We have also received another summons for Will after he was caught travelling on the railways without a ticket. He gives our address every time. Guy was furious that Will had been in the house – that he might have taken something – but Alex had locked the upstairs doors where most of our valuables are kept.

How did we get here? Don't ask questions; there are no answers. It's exhausting and goes nowhere. I asked Guy to phone William and reiterate that he must not come to the house uninvited, but Guy seemed reluctant to do it. He has a job which requires him to fight in court every day, and he doesn't want to come home to more fighting and confrontation. He's told me this before, and I do understand.

I am feeling angry with Guy, though, and I know he's angry with me, although he doesn't say so. But I can feel it. He so easily gets angry with Will's behaviour, which is understandable, but he seems to be observing me and my every move – to make sure I don't 'move over' into Will's camp. I feel I'm in the middle of the two of them, and have been for years. It's so tiring. When I'm firmly at Guy's side, turning my back on William, Guy is happier and secure with that. But he is always looking out for my change of heart and my impending betrayal of him. The whole thing is like a Greek tragedy being played out.

I know he's feeling betrayed by his own family and has done for some time. His mother has always appeared to prefer Will to anyone else in the entire family – make that in her entire world – and I know that has hurt Guy, especially when Will has done some appalling things that have not been recognized by his mother. Guy and his sister, Martha, are no longer in touch. Martha told Guy at Christmas, during a phone call about Will returning from their mother's, that it was wrong to have excluded William from the house, and that Guy needed to make more of an effort with his son. She became unable to speak without screaming, and handed the phone over to her husband to complete the conversation. They haven't spoken since. It was the day after that particular conversation that we found stolen goods in William's bag, so that has never been spoken about with Martha. Guy's mother knew about it, of course, because as you will remember there was a mirror that William had stolen from her among the things we found. As you will also remember, she responded to the situation by putting a large amount of money into William's account the next day, without reference to Guy or myself.

I know all of this is the cause of huge sadness to my husband, added to which I know that he feels he must have been an inadequate role model for his eldest son for him to have turned out this way. I have spent a lot of time trying to convince him otherwise, and he is able to run with this and always talks about his other boys, saying that his family don't mention how well they have turned out. It is always 'poor William'. I can't do a great deal about any of this, and when I'm tired I can do even less. I wish I could make it alright for Guy, but I can't. I've always tried to play the role of peacemaker; most of my life I've chosen that part in whatever 'play' I was in at the time, but I can't effect a change here. It's up to other players to write their own lines now. I give up on that.

Meanwhile, William has been asked to leave his house by the landlord. He says it is because of a mix-up over money, but who knows what the reasons are. I could guess they might include smoking weed in his room, leaving the TV on all night, not cleaning up, and general anti-social behaviour incompatible with communal living.

He texted me late on Saturday night, saying that he wanted to say goodbye forever, and was sorry he couldn't do so in person. He signed off, saying he loved me so much and was sorry he was such a disappointment to me.

Oh, right. So what do I do here? Nothing, I thought, switching off my phone and going to bed. I'm too tired. What's happening is that he's trying a different way to suck me in, and I won't be pulled into the madness any longer. Guy became angry that Will had sent such a text, and hardly slept that night.

Whilst I was in the shower the next morning, wondering what to do about the text, Jack rang William, and Guy spoke to him too. He was alive and with a friend on the other side of town. Guy told him that we were going to a pub in Greenwich if he wanted to join us for lunch. William didn't come, but did phone later and ask to speak to us privately, not in a public place. I agreed that he could come to the house, at which point Guy began saying that everyone dances to his tune and that it was 'here we go again'.

What do I do? I thought. This seemed right, asking him to come over if he needed to talk, but Guy sees me as a betrayer if I do. We sat outside in the garden. I asked Guy to sit with us. Will held his head in his hands and cried, saying that he needed to give up cannabis and that it was ruining his life.

'Not having a family is killing me,' he said. 'I can't do it any longer. I've got no friends and no prospects. My landlord wants me out in two weeks. I can't go on like this any more.'

We both talked to him about going into rehab, that he should go and see his counsellor and ask for her help. Guy went inside later to start preparing for the next day's case, and I stayed in the garden with Will. I brought out pens and paper so he could make a list of what he needed to do, then asked him to draw a map on large pieces of art paper, of where he would like to go with his life. He did this, and seemed calmer afterwards. He said he wouldn't go into rehab; he couldn't bear the thought of that again. But he said he won't ever do cannabis again. He's been using it as a painkiller, he said, and that's the hard part – when you're in pain, what do you substitute your painkiller with?

I don't know whether he can make the changes without going into rehab for a long time. We're certainly not paying for anything else. We've stopped giving him cash at all.

He came to the house yesterday, and used the internet to search for jobs, achieving an interview for that afternoon. I had to stand over him, almost, so that he wouldn't go checking in drawers for cheques or account numbers. I wish I knew how all of this was going to turn out, but I don't. We had a good day yesterday, though. Jack was off school and we went for lunch with William, who went to his interview afterwards. He rang me later sounding upbeat.

'Yeah, it went well,' he said. 'But, I'm the first one they've seen, and they're going to let me know. I know how to work behind a bar now, though, as they gave me a two-hour trial, so that's good experience for me.'

I haven't mentioned to Guy that William came to the house again. I don't want to create a bad atmosphere. If he asks me I'll tell him, but for now I think I'll just leave things as they are.

12 June

True or false

Will is still not smoking cannabis, or so he says, and I hope very much that's true. Everything is unravelling for him though, and it's confusing how calm he is about it. I know that cannabis smokers have a tendency to live in the present moment, and have difficulty in planning ahead. It is now Tuesday and he needs to vacate the house he is living in on Friday.

By the end of last week I became frazzled talking to him about this, when he didn't seem to see any urgency to the situation. His Job-seeker's allowance has been stopped, he says. Something to do with not declaring how many jobs he's been for. The housing benefit that was in place has also somehow dried up. Something about cheques being issued in the wrong name. He's been issued with an eviction notice by his landlord. So, essentially, the things that we urged and helped him to put in place when he moved out of B&B accommodation, are now disappearing. He has no job, either.

I'm feeling calmer about all of this at the moment, but last week felt so angry with him for mucking it all up. How is this possible? That really takes some doing. He had signed a lease on the house for six months, so there should have been peace at least until September, but now 'here we go again', to quote Guy.

I have just read an email from a drugs counsellor, who is a member of our campaign group. She was writing about the aspect of rebellion among young people, some of whom use drugs and drink as primary weapons of attack. She had spoken to a 21-year-old drug user only yesterday, who had said that he was not through with drugs yet, because he hadn't finished rebelling. At 21? Right. Useful information for me; I am now wondering whether, at 19, Will is still rebelling. After all, we helped Will move into his present house, and encouraged him to apply for benefits, hoping he could attain a level of independence that way, and achieve distance from us.

I haven't helped him find a new room this time, despite the urgency. Something has stopped me doing so – mainly boredom and utter frustration. The repetition of events is getting to me. However, I am convinced we're doing the right thing – this time if he mucks up it will be his own handiwork he'll be attacking and not ours. Hard for a mother not to want to get involved, but he's made it easier by completing similar circles for years now.

We met this morning. He had two interviews for jobs today. He seems to be getting interviews, but not jobs, and I have talked to him about it being a 'numbers game', as the recruiters call it. He seems to say the right things, acknowledges what I tell him, but then no results – so far. I was encouraging and helpful again this morning – last week I wasn't. Being the shrew disturbs me, but I think he needs the mirror held up to him and did so – again.

Our meeting took place this morning after he rang to ask if he could borrow an A-Z to find an address in central London. Guy is out of town and has taken the car. Both our street maps are in there, so I took Lily with me and went to meet Will at the bottom of the hill, and bought him a map at the local garage on the main thoroughfare from Lewisham to Deptford. Looking over at William, checking him out as I always do, I noticed he looked well – his blue eyes clear and sparkling – and told him so. He smiled and said he was keeping off the cannabis. He's made an appointment to see Sally, the drugs counsellor. I hope that's true because he's going to need support if he's not going to do rehab.

As we walked along, I told Will what Guy had said to me the day before, when he'd been talking about how he managed to kick smoking several years ago. He'd told himself that he was a smoker who was choosing not to smoke, and that had done it for him. Telling himself he was a non-smoker had produced a negative effect. Will nodded and said he could understand that. We went over the road to the café we'd been to before, and sat outside for half an hour, traffic thundering by. I held Lily on my lap, not wanting to put her down among the fag ends and chewing gum on the pavement. Out of the corner of my eye I could see smiles of approbation for her from passers-by. (Yesterday I came panting out of a shop I'd run into, after tying her up outside, with obvious misgivings, but I needed to buy milk for a later cup of PG Tips, to find a tourist taking her photo.) We talked about the interviews Will had coming up later in the day, and I heard myself laughing loudly at jokes he was making. The sun was out, and it was going to be a warm day. Even this area seemed quite pleasant in the sunshine, but what café these days doesn't have filter coffee? Come again? This place is as terrible as it looks on the outside. Surrendering to a cup of Nescafé, and toast spread with Stork margarine (What? are we back in the 1960s?), I listened to Will saying that he was sure he could find somewhere else to live by Friday. I reminded him that I was going away to visit my half-brother this weekend, so I couldn't help him move his things. 'No, I know. That's not a problem. I'll sort it out. I've still got a few days,' he said. I pushed the plate of toast over to him, and, examining it closely first, he ate half a slice.

In spite of my resolve, I heard myself asking if he needed any help with finding another place, because a few days isn't enough, and homelessness scares me. Then, as I was walking away with Lily, waving and wishing him luck, I decided again that because of the issue of rebellion I would let him do things himself this time. We'll almost certainly have to pay the deposit and another month's rent, but that's because we need to sleep at night.

Whilst sitting on a grassy knoll in Greenwich Park half an hour later, throwing a ball for Lily, I sent him a text to wish him luck with his 11 o'clock interview. It was for a bar job at a pub near Covent Garden. He rang later to say he thought they'd liked him, and they had said they would call tomorrow. I hope this is true, too. Last week he told me he was working in a club in Mayfair, which proved to be fantasy. We've talked about trying always to tell the truth, but who knows. He sounded happy on the phone, and hopeful. I smiled and looked around at the large oak trees silhouetted against the blue sky, as I listened to him. It's good for me to have to walk with Lily every morning; we almost always go into the park, which is at its most beautiful now. There is every hue of green here, and the roses are in bloom. Being close to the trees, in particular, some of which are centuries old, is very grounding for me. I need to remember that I can be as solid as they are: when the high winds begin I need to be as firmly rooted as one of these. It is a good image for me, as I head towards a possibly stormy few weeks ahead.

29 June

Snakes and ladders

I've been busy trying to keep everything going here – including myself. I suppose the first thing to say is that Alex has been visibly upset at school, breaking down in tears twice now.

I was called in to talk to the two Lower School heads last week, who wanted to know more about what was happening at home. Alex had told them something of the problems we have been having over the past years. They were surprisingly sympathetic. After I had stopped talking, I looked over at one of the men and away again quickly after noticing tears in his eyes. Both of them remembered William, and asked if he had begun smoking cannabis at their school, and where I thought that he had first obtained it. They seemed ready to admit that it was a problem for all schools and that it needed careful attention. I took the opportunity to tell them what I was doing to help raise awareness of skunk and smoking in childhood years. I was pleased to see that both of them seemed up to speed with the damage that it can do. They were also very supportive of Alex, wanting to help and asking me what I thought they could do.

The week before, Alex had explained that he felt he might turn out like William. He was sitting in the kitchen, still in school uniform, telling me that he had been crying that day at school. Looking at him as he spoke, I found it hard to empathize at first, wondering why he should be thinking this way. I don't think he and Will are alike in any way, so what was going on?

'I'm about the same age as he was when it all began, or near enough

– I'll be in Year 9 next year, which is around the time… I go to the same school, he's my brother and some teachers have said how alike we are. What if I start to become like him, and begin stealing and going crazy?'

Turning to put the kettle on, and asking him if he'd like a cuppa, I listened as Alex went on to say that he just needed to talk.

I made tea, and sat down at the kitchen table opposite him. He was looking down at his hands, explaining how awful it felt to be thinking these thoughts. Alex, my sweet boy.

Part of the picture here is that William had come to the door the week before saying he had nothing to eat, and this had upset Alex more than I'd thought. We have not been giving him cash, only supermarket gift vouchers. I had seen him earlier that day and had said I would buy him another voucher; he had said he had no food in his fridge. Later on at home, I had begun to feel unwell, so drained, my head aching; I'd decided that it would have to wait until the next day. I didn't want to get back in the car to drive to the supermarket.

We had told Will that he must not come to the house without being invited, but that's what he did. Jack opened the door to him and told him that I wasn't well and that he should go.

I could hear William crying, saying that we were abandoning him, pushing past Jack and refusing to go when asked, saying that he needed food. He sat on the step inside the front door as Jack closed it, refusing to move. Saying that we needed to sort this out, Jack grabbed a plastic bag and began filling it from the fridge. Will went then. It was later that same week that Will had sent me the text saying goodbye forever, and two days later, that he needed to talk to us. He later told us that he was determined to give up cannabis, agreeing once again that it was ruining his life. I told both Alex and Jack, after the stand-off on the door step, that I would talk again to Will about coming to the house uninvited, and this would not happen again. I would make sure of that.

The good news is that after this episode that clearly upset Alex so much, William seemed motivated to stop smoking and to get a job, which he did. It was Friday morning, two weeks ago; I was getting ready to go up to Herefordshire for the weekend with my sister to see our younger half-brother and his partner, when William rang me to say he'd got a full-time job in a pub in St James's. He was so excited he could hardly speak. I told him to slow down and tell me the details. It had to be true, he sounded so genuinely euphoric.

I told him that he had done this by himself, and how wonderful that was.

'Yeah, well, I did - but I couldn't have done it without you in the background helping me, though. I knew I could do it. Someone's said "yes" after all the interviews I've been for. I can get off benefits now. Yes! I've done it. I can start again and put everything behind me. Yes! Oh, I just feel so amazing.'

I looked around the hallway as I listened to him talk, coats and shoes lying expectantly, waiting to be chosen for packing. I breathed slowly and deeply and said a silent 'thank you' to a universe that had become such an inflexible teacher. Here was a reward for his working hard to get a job. He had still to find somewhere to live, though. The day he got his job, that day, was also the day he had been told to vacate his room. I talked to him about this, and he said he'd found a room in a house in Blackheath village, about ten minutes away from where we are. Apparently, he had told his present landlord that he would move out in the early part of the next week, a few days after his eviction notice, and that the landlord was cool with that. There was no problem, he said. I was unsure how the timing would work out, but decided to trust it all, because Will seemed very relaxed.

Will began working the following Monday. His landlord rang me that evening to say that he had cleared out Will's room and had his things – they were in the back of the car and could he bring them over? 'Oh, I suppose so,' I began saying. As the car drew up ten minutes later and the landlord began to carry black bin-liners of clothes and books to our door, I wondered where Will was going to sleep that night. I rang him. He was at work, saying he couldn't understand why his stuff had been taken from his room; he had nowhere to sleep now.

Alex had had another outburst at school. We had just finished talking about how William would never live with us again, that Alex could be assured that even if things didn't work out with Will's job he would always live away from us because his behaviour was too damaging. Now, here I was only minutes later, at 6 o'clock in the evening, with Will's stuff in the hallway, and my promise to Alex echoing in my head. Of course he never would – but tonight? If Will had nowhere else to go – what should I do?

I knew that Guy was going into a meeting at 6 pm, so he was not contactable. He would be furious about this whole situation. He had been angry for months now; this was more ammunition for his already overcrowded arsenal. When Will rang me again later I said that he should come to our house after work, which was going to be around midnight, and sleep at our house that night.

Guy rang me then, and when I explained what had happened, he asked me what I thought I was doing telling Will he could stay. He rang Will and told him not to come to the house. He was right, but homelessness scares me, especially when Will had only just that day begun a new job, which I was praying he could hang onto. But, I knew I couldn't win on this one.

Guy hardly spoke to me that night. He said he couldn't understand how I could have made that decision. He then sat down in the sitting room with his meal, and began laughing loudly at *Frasier*. I went to bed alone, wondering how he could be so cruel to me.

However, Will did have a job. Two days later we helped him move into his new place, a shared house in Blackheath village. Things seemed more certain than they had for months. I had also persuaded Guy that he and I needed to get some counselling support together. We went to see the therapist that has been helping me these past few years. She is an expert in addictions, and had offered to see us, together, many months before.

I had been talking to my sister on the telephone about the strain on my relationship with Guy, and she told me that most couples who have similar issues split up, because they blame each other. She cited a few high-profile cases, like the family of Stephen Lawrence, whose parents had separated. What? As I put the phone down to her, Guy rang me from Sussex where he was working. He sounded very cheerful, and loving. This was a pattern though; he usually left his smile at the garden gate when he came home in the evenings.

I told him what my sister had just said, and managed to get him to agree to come with me to a counselling session. We made an appointment for the next week, and went along. It was enormously useful, one of my better ideas. We talked about William, and what the trauma and loss had meant to both of us. I listened as Guy talked about his feelings, and something happened in that room that day. Guy seemed to leave some of his cares in there, and came away lighter and happier than I'd seen him in a long time. So far, he has remained in that space.

We discussed with the therapist our concerns about Alex and Jack. Guy said he needed a break from Will – that when he comes home at night he doesn't know what to expect, and needs to think about the other members of the family, that we've spent too much time trying to get Will back on track, and that it was time now to look after ourselves – as a separate unit.

We decided that the way forward should be that we would tell Will that he should not come to the house for three months. The therapist advised us that we needed this amount of time for the recovery of the four of us. She told us that we needed to ensure Alex did not try and get comfort elsewhere – either through drugs, alcohol or even latching onto another family. He needed time to relax and breathe, as we all did. This seemed like a good solution, one which I could see working. This decision would be reviewed in October, and we would continue to meet Will away from the house, on a regular basis.

We told Will that weekend what we had decided, and he seemed to take it well. We asked him what support he needed from us, and he said he needed nothing. Guy bought him groceries, though, and a supermarket voucher so he could feed himself for another week. We also bought him a travelcard so he could get to work.

It would appear, though, that Will has since left his job. He rang me late on Sunday night to say that he had bumped into his ex-girlfriend over the weekend and he was unsure whether he could go through life knowing how much he had stolen off her, and how he'd hurt her. He said he couldn't understand why he'd smoked so much draw and become a thief, how crazy it all was, and now he was having to live with it. We talked about making changes, and how he could look forward, and how useless an emotion guilt was. He was very low, and I tried my best to say how well he had done getting a job and moving into a new place – all of which he had accomplished himself. I also talked about how the bad times are like compost for growth – the more shit you throw on flowers the better they do and it's the same for our own growth – it's only in the bad times that you really learn anything. We talked until the early hours, and I offered to meet him for breakfast the next day. He said he wanted a lie-in, so I said I'd call him in the morning, before he set off for work, which I did but got no reply.

He rang me much later and said he still felt awful, and could we meet after all, but I said I couldn't do that. We arranged to meet for breakfast the next day, Tuesday, but he didn't turn up. He wasn't answering his phone, either, but rang me two days later, yesterday, asking to meet for coffee. Something in me wants to leap and help him automatically, and I virtually dropped everything, including our puppy, and drove over to his house in the village. As I was reaching for the car keys, though, I hurriedly tore open a letter which was from the landlord of Will's old flat. We had asked for the balance of the deposit to be sent to us.

It wasn't a cheque, though, but a letter saying that William's room had been in a 'disgusting state' and that there would be a charge for cleaning it, and replacing the mattress which had 'usually been slept on without a sheet'. Memories of trying to clear out the flat in Streatham that Will had rented with a friend, this time last year, surfaced. We had paid £500 deposit that time, of which none was returned. I can still smell the foul stench of that place when we went to clear Will's things out the day he was admitted to the Priory Hospital.

We had to give up trying to clean that flat; it was too big a job. There had been dirty clothes everywhere, and evidence of drug use in every room, along with used condoms and cigarette butts littering every inch of floor. There were cobwebs on the stairs, something I'd never seen anywhere before. As I read the landlord's letter, the refrain 'here we go again and why can't he behave like normal people' began to strike its first notes. Closing my eyes to calm myself, I could feel anger begin punching holes in my stomach, even though I had missed Will this week and wanted to see him.

As we sat down in a coffee shop in Blackheath village and started talking, I began to feel that Will was lying to me again. He said he wasn't working, and hadn't been for two days, because a wall had fallen down outside the pub. He would be going in later. The conversation continued to decline after this. We had paid off his overdraft at the bank – he had originally said that someone was 'scamming' his account, and we had settled the amount, you will remember – with the proviso that he would close the account, and not begin to run up another overdraft.

We began to talk about that account now: he was saying that he didn't want to close it because his employer needed somewhere to bank his wages, which he wouldn't get for another month, incidentally. I asked him if he had money, and he said that I was the one with the money – he didn't have any. He hadn't signed on either, so no benefits were in place any more.

I began to feel very angry, and flounced out telling him he was full of crap, and drove home. I rang the pub he'd said he worked for when I got back. It turns out he had worked for four days last week, and hadn't returned again this week. I rang him then, saying I wanted to give him the opportunity to tell me the truth. He said that seeing his ex-girlfriend had upset him too much, he couldn't go back. ('You don't understand the pain I'm in.') I screamed at him then, and slammed the phone down. Despair, again. Part of me was glad the job had existed at all, because there was always an outside chance he had been lying about that too. I had tried to help him, by sorting out things for him to wear for his first week, and washing all his clothes that had been dumped here – everything had been dirty, so I had taken the whole lot down to the launderette.

Now, he hadn't continued with it. Something I knew he'd been so happy to get. But, thinking about it, he had been unable to do one day a week at college – so it was optimistic to think he could do a job. I hadn't liked the look of his eyes when I met him yesterday. Although he appeared clean, his eyes looked drugged and dull.

It feels like this is the end of something. Both Guy and I had believed that if our son could find a job, he might find self-respect and would enjoy having his own money, and his life would begin to get better – and ours too. But, he had found a job, one which he seemed to enjoy, and now this. An ongoing nightmare is what it feels like. I am determined that he is on his own now. If he wants to lie in bed and not work then he's going to have to fund his own life, and sort things out for himself. He had a chance to get his life on track. The irony is that I have recently had two good, long telephone conversations with him. I am impressed each time by how intelligent he is, how informed and also how emotionally literate. I don't know what this means; it doesn't make any sense. I don't know what the future holds, how many times you can ride this particular rollercoaster without it making you sick.

It is a matter of priorities now. My highest priorities are my other two boys, who need care after what they have been through, and keeping our family safe. My other priority is the wider picture, and the campaign to help make sure that this cannabis epidemic does not affect the next generation of children and families as it has this one. It is a public scandal that so many families are afflicted because cannabis is seen as a safe, cool drug. Tony Blair's Government let us down when they reclassified this drug; as parents we have been undermined. What chance did we have of persuading our children away from this evil? We have a new Government; I'm determined that they listen to us, those of us who are watching our children destroy themselves.

13 July

Getting things done, moving fast

Things with the Action Group are going well. We are determined to make the Government aware of the extensive suffering that is taking place among families across the country, due to cannabis misuse among children and teens. We have no one political party allegiance; our intention is to get cross-party support in Parliament, to make change happen. I have asked everyone who is on our mailing list to go and see their own MP, to talk about the effect that cannabis is having on family life.

We now have support from a number of MPs, some of whom we have approached, others who have expressed an interest in meeting us. We have been to see Tim Loughton, the Shadow Health and Children's Minister, who now supports our group. Edward Garnier MP, Graham Brady MP and Christopher Chope MP have all said they support our group too. Our core steering group is made up of parents, all of whom have personal experience of the misery that cannabis can cause. We also have a large group of advisers alongside us, including: biologist and Eurad spokesperson, Mary Brett; Anthony Seldon, Master of Wellington College; Peter Stalker, who heads the NDPA; Peter Walker, an ex-headteacher who advises on drugs-testing across the world; and James Langton, from the Clearhead organization.

I don't think the Government foresaw what a disaster the downgrading decision would be for families: as I will never tire of saying, reclassification sent out the confused message to the public that it was safe to smoke cannabis. Children began using it as part of their adolescent rebellion. It isn't cigarettes children are smoking behind bike-sheds now, it's cannabis, and mainly skunk, and it is driving thousands of them wild.

We are putting a petition on the website in the next few days and we will need as many people as possible to sign it. We can then show it to the Government, as proof of how many people feel strongly about the issues. The main points are these:

- Firstly, the public need to be made aware of the scientific and medical facts about the potential effects of cannabis (particularly skunk) on the mental health of children and teenagers.
- Secondly, we'd like to see preventative drug-education in schools, using powerful marketing techniques.
- Thirdly, we would like to see the law changed and reclassification of cannabis back to Class B from Class C, to send out the powerful, unequivocal message that smoking cannabis in childhood and teen years is highly dangerous.

People will be asked to sign via email. Sounds like a good idea? I hope so.

I have been to the launch of the Conservative Party's *Social Justice Policy Group Report* this week, and the findings are fascinating. Although I have no allegiance to any political party, I am delighted that this report has been published, bringing the UK's huge social problems into the spotlight.

Drugs are, of course, among the most difficult social issues with which this country is faced. We have the worst record in Western Europe. How did that happen? There is a lot of talk about the 'war on drugs' but I don't think that war has ever started. As someone at yesterday's meeting at the launch of the Addictions Working Party document said, there is too much tolerance of drugs – we do not need them as a society. What we need are policies of zero tolerance, and we need to protect children from the ills of drugs by raising their awareness so that they don't start using them in the first place.

Cannabis, though, is still seen as a cool, soft, harmless drug. The generation who smoked it back in college, who are now in their late forties and their fifties, have added to the problem that is now afflicting so many of us, by their belief that cannabis is harmless. Indeed, the baby-boomers, some of whom are still smoking cannabis, are now running the country. But back in the sixties and seventies, people weren't smoking cannabis until later, in their twenties usually. Children and teens were certainly not smoking the stuff en masse, and the cannabis that was on sale was generally resin which is not as strong as the home-grown skunk that kids are smoking now.

All the medical evidence is there to underline the dangers of smoking this super-strength, hydroponically cultivated substance in childhood. Everyone who smokes it will be affected in some way; those who become habitual users may never recover. I have had three mothers write to me this week, signing up to our campaign, who have lost their sons to cannabis. Children are dying, and this is cannabis we are talking about. Some kids become depressed and can't keep their lives together; others move on to alcohol and/or harder drugs and lose their lives that way. Siblings are suffering; I had one mother write to me today to say that her youngest son is having suicidal thoughts; her eldest son died from a heroin overdose after beginning on cannabis at 13. She is devastated, and talked to me of the anger she feels at the selfishness of drug addicts, who only see their own needs, not realizing that everyone around them is affected.

Within my own family, Alex has been talking to us again about his feelings around what has happened to us as a family. He is happy to have broken up from school. He did not do well in his exams, and will be in one of the lowest streamed classes next year, from being in the highest. I try to tell myself that he will be fine next year, but feel guilty about the amount of attention I have given to Will and his problems, presuming Alex would do well at his studies as he is a very able child.

At least Will is no longer in the house, nor will he ever live here again, so maybe we can restore a sense of peace which will enable Alex to thrive, and to relax and blossom at school. He is still upset and fragile, though, and has asked that we treat him like a child, not a grown-up. He says he hasn't wanted to talk to us about how he's been feeling, so as not to add to our burden, but he's now embarrassed about breaking down at school and crying and says he doesn't entirely trust that we won't have Will back. He says that some kids at school make fun of him for having a brother who is a drug addict, and he says that's normal, that's what happens, but people don't understand what it's been like.

Alex's mugging back in April seems to have been the trigger for his nervousness and his need to talk about the effects of living with a brother like Will. Having his phone and iPod taken by the muggers brought back memories of Will taking his belongings, sometimes going into his room late at night, when he was in bed. Alex is clearly wounded by what he has been through. He is a big, robust boy, though, and acts and speaks much older than his years, so that can be confusing for those who come into contact with him. We need to remember, that he is only 13, and, as he says, he was only eight or nine when our problems at home began, hardly even knowing what cannabis was. He says that Jack also takes out his aggression on him, which upsets him.

Will is still in his house in Blackheath, but I have not spoken to him for a week. He told me that he was going to try to get his job back, by explaining that he had been ill and that that was why he had left and not returned. I am not sure what has happened on that front.

Caroline, Guy's mother, came to stay with us last weekend. It was Open Day at Alex's school, and since the time that Will was first at that school she (and Guy's father, when he was alive) would always come up for that event. This year it was raining heavily as I dropped Alex off. Women in lacy finery were stepping around puddles like lakes in high-heeled sling-backs, the men struggling to open golfing umbrellas against the wind. Guy had arranged to meet his mother in London and then travel down to Alex's school in south-east London together. Guy's relationship with his mother, and consequently with his sister, has been different since Will went to stay at her house last winter, after we had made the decision to exclude him again. Both Guy's sister and mother have over the years alluded to the fact that we have been too strict as parents, and consequently Will cannot be accountable for what he's done.

Will was still at his crammer in Kensington when he went to live with Caroline, making a third attempt to complete A levels, as you will remember. Guy's sister, Martha, was not happy that Will was staying with her mother, but it was Caroline who had offered Will accommodation. He had been 'sofa-surfing' since we had thrown him out over the October half-term holiday, after the repeated thefts and drug-induced aggression that were affecting us all. I think my mother-in-law felt that she could do a better job than us. He was to commute from her house in Surrey to central London every day, a journey of around an hour.

'I'm giving him a lot of TLC, you know – really looking after him. I think it's good for his soul,' she told me just after he had arrived.

I wished her luck, saying that it wasn't a lack of care that Will was suffering from, but skunk addiction, but I was unconvinced that she had heard me, or understood what that meant. I hardly understood it myself, but knew that we couldn't continue with Will in our midst.

At that time, Will had been stealing from just about everyone he came into contact with. When Guy drove Will down to his mother's home, an hour and a half away from our house, in Surrey, on a cold October evening, he took our safe with him, calmly showing his mother how to use it, telling her not to leave the code number lying around. (No, of course, dear, don't you worry, I won't. He'll be fine with me. I've never had any trouble with him.)

Guy said it seemed a bizarre thing to be doing. It was in that house that Will and Jack had spent a lot of time when they were little, staying with their grandparents, and now Guy was dropping Will there just as we used to do years ago, but this time under the appalling circumstances that we could no longer have him in our house, and with a safe under his arm. It is also the house that Guy spent his childhood; he was born there.

Will was there for six weeks. We knew that Caroline would be under a strain having Will in the house. Even an 'ordinary' teenager in your house when you're 80 would be hard-going, but she was not admitting anything to us. Her game-plan was, I'm sure, that the arrangement with her would be such a success that we would be encouraged to have him back to start again. ('He's never been any trouble with me' was becoming her catch-phrase, along with 'I do give him money though; do you give him money? Because London is very expensive. That's probably the problem – that he doesn't have enough money, so he takes it.')

We heard from Guy's sister, however, that Caroline had been complaining to her about the worry Will was causing her: not coming home when he said he would so she would often wait up for him or change her plans to accommodate him only to find it had not been necessary. He was also disappearing for days at a time, she often lying awake at night wondering where he was. I remember many telephone conversations with Caroline where we said that if it was too much, we would arrange for Will to go elsewhere. She wouldn't admit there was a problem, though, but told us repeatedly that he needed to be with his family. We agreed, but were unsure how you integrate someone into a family who so clearly doesn't want to be there, and told her this.

'But he misses all of you so much,' she said.

'Does he? Has he said so?'

'No, but I'm sure he does. He should be with his family. He's been fine with me, no trouble at all.'

I took this to mean that if he was no trouble with her, then he should be no trouble with us. If only that were true. The one thing I knew I wanted back then was to have my family intact again. I still do, but have given up the hope of Will ever living with us. At that time, and until very recently, I still held out the hope that Will could live with us without contravening what few rules we had within 24 hours of his being in the house, which was the pattern.

My impression is that Caroline is a highly competitive woman; she needs to win at whatever she's doing. The story is still that Will was fine when he was with her, even though the truth is somewhat different. Even after we found the mirror belonging to her in Will's jeans, the day he returned to us after living with her, she found it difficult to acknowledge the truth of what was going on. Maybe she wants to be the good cop to our bad one.

As you will remember, William was with her when he stole a mobile phone from a table in a restaurant. But this is not referred to, either, almost as though if you don't look at it, it doesn't exist. That is one way of viewing the world, I suppose, and I understand it is an attitude that is of its time. My own birth family acted in a similar way to adversity. I know also that Caroline's mission when she became a grandmother was to be like her own granny, who lived with her when she was young, and with whom she had a particularly close bond, unlike with her mother. She told me this when William was born. She wanted to be well loved and well thought of by her grandchildren so that people would speak kindly about her after she had died, she said.

Last weekend, though, she was in danger of not being thought of in those terms by her own son, certainly. Guy told me later that one of the first things she said to him when they arrived at Open Day was that it was Will's birthright to live at home.

'Not if he's trying to destroy it, it's not,' Guy had replied.

They both stared out grimly at the pouring rain from the Pimm's tent. Guy said he wanted to scream then, but instead told her about Alex. Maybe this would make her see what the truth was.

'Alex is really suffering. He's broken down twice at school and is seeing the counsellor. Deb's been called in to see the teachers, who are worried about him. They've been asking what they can do to help, as it's obvious Alex is in some distress.'

'He looks alright to me,' she replied.

She gave Alex £50 in cash, later, which certainly made him smile. If only things could really be fixed so easily with money.

14 August

Finding a way through

Guy and I came home from holiday at the weekend. We had spent a week in Sicily with Alex, and then a few days in London, before driving up to the Suffolk coast for a further week. Jack was in Turkey with a friend and his family whilst we were in Italy, but came to Suffolk. We had asked William if he wanted to join us this year, but he'd declined. He remained at his house in Blackheath, and for the first time in four years, he didn't invade our house or do anything which would cause problems when we got home.

For the past three years we have asked our cleaning lady, Phoebe, to house-sit, after coming home to chaos the year William was doing GCSEs. He was supposed to be staying with a friend's family, but you'll recall he broke into the house and lived there instead for a prolonged weed-fest, abandoning the place the day we returned.

Last year he was supposed to be coming to Italy with us, after returning home from rehab, but lost his passport the day before we were due to travel. (We now think he had sold it.) So, we arranged for him to stay with his grandmother instead. He stayed with her for a couple of days and then came back to London to live in the house with Phoebe, even though we had told him he should not be there without us.

We saw Will on Sunday the day after we got back from Suffolk, and the meeting did not go well. I hadn't seen him since before we'd gone to Sicily. I had been ill on holiday there, after foolishly deciding to eat some fish. We were staying by the sea and the freshly caught fish all looked so wonderful, but I hadn't eaten meat or fish for five or six years, and the effect made me feel very ill. I was still suffering once back in London. We had arranged to meet Will for a drink locally before we set off for Suffolk, but I was feeling unwell and Guy was working, so it didn't happen.

Will had rung me while we were in Suffolk. I was having a bad day, and clearly he was too. We were renting the same house that we've been taking for the past nine years, with the exception of last year when the letting was transferred to an agent, who booked the entire summer out before we could put in our request again. Standing in the hallway on our first day back there, Guy looked unhappy and began talking about the memories that the place held for him: noisy family holidays when all three boys would be with us, including grandparents and friends at different times over the years. It seemed odd to him, he said, that it was so quiet there now. No William, and Jack had asked to stay in London a few days more, so that he could catch up with friends.

Guy had clearly been in an agitated state before we left for Suffolk. Sicily had been a great success, but tiring in the searing heat. He had work to do before we left again for Suffolk, and the day we left London we heard that a friend of ours had died during the night. She had been ill for over a year, with bowel cancer, and it had been a cruel disease which she had fought hard to overcome.

Guy looked at me, in silence first, then said, 'Yeah, life's a bitch, and then you die, don't you?'

I could feel a heavier energy enter the kitchen where we were both standing, and silently feared that he would start to become depressed as a result of the news. I can feel how sensitive he is, this death adding to his take on life that he's been dealt a heavy blow from which he is still reeling. I have relied on him to prop me up so often over the years, mainly around my ongoing grief and pain from having had a difficult start in life. Now it seems it's my turn; we have changed places.

Guy has always loved going to the house in Suffolk, which is on Iken Cliff, not far from Orford, overlooking the beach and the mud flats which extend to the Snape Maltings. The house used to be a pub, dating from the seventeenth century, set in over an acre of land, once at the heart of a thriving agricultural community which vanished long ago.

I was dismayed this year to find that Guy continued to seem sad and disturbed, instead of calm and smiling, which is the usual effect on him of being up there. Even the view of Iken Church in the distance only seemed to have a temporary glow for him.

One of the things that happens when Guy is becoming low is that he seems to want to control everything, including me. If I have an idea for something, his first response is 'no' plus some reason why it's a bad idea. This is wearing and hurtful for me, and I began to notice it more and more whilst we were away. He had to be in charge; what he said needed to be rigidly adhered to. I can see why he does this: it's a response to feeling out of control with life itself, and who can blame him? His eldest son being the way he is, and witnessing his mother and sister tying their colours firmly to William's mast, Guy must feel as if his world no longer makes sense. Add to that a wife who is going out into the world trying to make changes, and you have a recipe for unrest.

Fine, I could see that, but was unsure how I was going to stop myself being wounded by his behaviour towards all of us, and began to feel that I didn't know how to keep going in that climate, especially as I was verging on exhaustion myself. I became aware that I was trying to keep tears at bay, which is unlike me. I told Guy something of how I was feeling one morning on holiday as we sat outside having breakfast, Lily running around us one minute, and off exploring woodland and bushes the next. Guy took the criticism badly and refused to acknowledge what I was saying.

'Oh, good, just blame me for everything if that makes you feel better. It's my fault, that's right.'

Things became worse from there on, and I began to be thoroughly out of sorts with everything. Then William rang me, telling me he just wanted to say hello. (Oh, okay, yes I'm alright, we're in Suffolk. How are you?) He rang back again five minutes later, to say that he was panicking about money and needed help.

'I'm only a teenager. I don't have a clue about money. My old landlord owes me hundreds of pounds which I could use to pay my rent this month, but he won't answer my calls. Do you have a mobile number for him? Yeah, that's why I rang before, to get that. I really need help.'

I began to say, unhelpfully, that I thought he had the rent. He had told us some weeks before, at one of the weekly meetings we've been having with him, that he had housing benefit back in place even though he was no longer signing on, which had sounded odd to me. Now it would seem that was another lie. He'd also recently told us that he had a weekend job, and we were unsure whether that was right or not. The truth was that his grandmother had given him a lump sum of money, and he was living off that, not working or signing on.

I said that he needed to get a full-time job so he could begin to support himself.

'You don't get it, do you? You tell me how awful I am, what a useless son I am to you, and how crap I am, and you don't understand it's not that easy just to get a job. I've had one and I fucked it up, like I do with everything.'

'Well, maybe it wasn't the right thing for you. You can try something else… '

Will began yelling more loudly, shouting over me as I was trying to talk. It seemed simple to me: if you need money for rent and aren't working, then you get a job – apparently not that simple for him.

More shouting down the phone, more panic in his voice. We've been here before; he's feeling bad and wants to dump it on someone.

'William, I'm going to have to go. I'll call you back later,' I said heavily, and pulled down the flap on my phone to end the call.

I was in the house by myself. It was a warm day and Guy had taken Alex and Jack to play tennis at Orford rec, about ten minutes away by car. We were hardly speaking, both of us angry and upset. Putting my phone down on the desk in the dining room, I walked out into the garden, through the conservatory with its cache of spiders, and sat down heavily on the sun-lounger I'd placed there minutes before. The house has a beautiful cottage garden, overlooking the beach, with tall blousy flowers at this time of year. Bees and butterflies love it, and looking around me now I wondered how things had got like this. Now Guy and I were fighting – more fragmentation – how easy it was to become disconnected with each other and to begin to look for other solutions than becoming connected again. Maybe I would be better off on my own, I began thinking; at least then I wouldn't have to deal with other people's moods. It wasn't fair. I felt like I was drowning.

My phone, which I'd left in the house, began to ring again – twice. Will.

I couldn't bring myself to speak to him. He clearly needed someone to yell at. Five minutes later, still trying to find a regular breathing rhythm again, I walked back into the house, picked up my phone and punched in his number. Will immediately apologized, and I quickly explained to him that I was having a bad day, and it wasn't a good time for me or his father at the moment. Then something extraordinary began to happen. Will started explaining to me in fast, breathless sentences, what it must have been like for his father these past few years – how the strain of having to deal with his eldest son's behaviour, coupled with the huge personal changes that I had made in my life must have been, at times, intolerable for Guy.

I started to smile, as I listened, and began to enjoy, and to be helped by, what he was saying. His slant on what it must be like to be Guy was fascinating, and made a lot of sense. There was no blame there, but an analysis that seemed to come from a place in our son which is clearly highly developed but to which we rarely have access. It is such a puzzle. But he did help me that day. I spoke to him until the credit silently ran out on my phone, and I suddenly found I was speaking only to myself. Staring into the impassive phone blankly, wondering how that had happened, I then rang him back from the house phone, but he didn't pick up. By the time Guy returned with the other boys, I was feeling nourished by my conversation with William, aware of the irony of this and surprised to find myself in a place of compassion for Guy, having been able to transform anger into tranquility in my heart, which I could then extend to everyone else.

The next morning I talked to Guy about what it was like for him regarding William. He said that as a father it was terrible to watch your eldest son become as he had. He talked about how lovely William was when he was little and how painful the memories were of being in Suffolk years ago, recalling William as a little boy running around in his football strip.

'I keep going over in my mind what happened. Was it to do with his height, do you think? He used to call himself a freak. That's a terrible word to use about yourself. As a father I feel I've failed. It must be my fault, something I did or didn't do. I know my family believe that. My mother has always been disapproving of me, and such a social climber. I was miserable at prep school, but she loved the place. I was never intellectual enough for my father either, a disappointment. Both of them were critical of our parenting, saying I was too strict. Maybe they were right, except that I always think about Jack and Alex, and what great young men they are both turning out to be. That really helps me. I know I can't be that bad a father, or they would be off the rails too, and so far there is no sign of that.'

On our drive back to London, as we were approaching the Dartford Bridge, its flexing multi-coloured vertebrae of slowly progressing cars shining in the distance, Guy turned to me and asked if I thought we should try and see William the next day. His concern is that if we don't arrange to see him, then he might begin to come to the house again. I had told Guy something of how lucid and helpful William had been on the phone, being careful how I worded this. Guy had nodded, and to my relief had not become angry. Looking puzzled, he said that that was part of the tragedy: that he was highly intelligent – much more so than either of us – and yet his talents were being wasted.

We met William the next day, at a wine bar in Blackheath. He was unshaven, and the haircut he had mentioned at every one of our weekly meetings ('I've got an appointment to have my hair cut. How do you think I should have it?') didn't seem to have happened. I was feeling irritated and tired. Guy was still trying to control everything and I was virtually at tipping point, but trying to hang on. Glancing at William's eyes I registered a familiar greyness I always associate with cannabis.

Sitting down with Will, whilst Guy went to the bar to buy drinks, I remembered fondly our conversation from the week before, but didn't mention it.

'So, you okay?' Will said to me, smiling.

We spoke for a few minutes, me asking how things were going, but what he said was almost exactly what he had said the week before, and the week before that. A trial for a weekend job now, when he'd said he had one already, thoughts about going abroad to work, but nothing concrete to report. Feeling angrily reckless, I said, 'God, Will, sounds like we're in a time-warp. You've been saying exactly the same things for weeks. What are you exactly doing with your time?'

'What was the point of that?' an internal voice began.

God knows, but I'm sick of the lies, and the pretence, came the silent reply.

Things inevitably went badly from there. I began asking questions in order to get at the truth. Me: 'Well, are you working or not?' Him: 'What do you think is the truth then? Do you think I am or not? I've fucked up everything. You blame everything on skunk but I'm not smoking, so explain that one. You expect me to do a full-time job, but when would I see my friends if I did that?' Madness.

Will became even more angry and then left, saying that he got nothing out of meeting us so what was the point? I agreed with him. Oh God, how was I going to cope with all of this? Guy being angry and difficult, now Will who was obviously still lying to us, saying he had a job, saying he'd applied to go abroad to work in September, saying he had housing benefit in place to pay this month's rent. I didn't believe any of it.

As we walked away I turned to Guy and said that we needed to know what was the situation between Will and his grandmother. We knew that she had given him some money to live on. I'd been saying that it was between the two of them what happened, but I felt I needed to know how much had been given. Will's mood was reminiscent of every other time that he had had money and then felt he could be rude to us, not caring what the outcome was. If his needs were met, in the short term, he would be careless with us. I presumed that that was the case now.

Guy phoned his mother as I was still kicking off my shoes in the hallway. He was told that she had paid this month's rent for Will, which was curious since Guy and our other two boys had spent the previous day with her, and she hadn't mentioned William. This is usually a sign that she has spoken to or seen her grandson, and almost always handed out cash. As Guy says, she uses her handbag as an answer to everything.

She had recently given Will £500 in cash and paid his rent, she said.

We went to our friend's funeral on Tuesday. Something moved Guy, and he began to make changes in his thinking, which is timely. I was unsure how much more depression and anger I could take. I'd been fighting back tears, feeling fragile and worn out since we'd come home. Jane, at 55, was only seven years older than us – the message for Guy was clear. He took my hand after the service, and said that he had decided to let go of all the pain around William. It was too hard he said, and the pressure of it all could end up killing both of us.

'I think it's time we both had some fun,' he said, looking into my eyes. What I saw there was a light that I hadn't seen for a long time. 'I've had enough of the heartache; it's only going to shorten both our lives, and that's not fair on us or our other boys. I'm letting go now. I've made a decision. I've tried to help Will, and I can't. I'm going to let him and my mother get on with it. I'm letting it all go.'

Oh, wow, what a gift for me and our other boys, too. Thanks, Jane.

Due to go back to work the next day, Guy took the rest of the week off, and has been more relaxed than I've seen him in years.

10 September

Just when you thought...

Guy and I have been to another counselling session, which was even more transformative than the last.

When we returned from holiday, I was certain that one of the first things we should do was book an appointment with Jana, to see us both as soon as possible. Guy's response to another appointment made me smile, as he began saying that probably at the end of September he would have some time free. Er, no, I replied, I was thinking more like tomorrow and if not then, definitely this week. He agreed.

I first went to Jana when I became ill five years ago. I was having panic attacks day and night, my left arm and leg were numb most of the time, and my heart rhythm seemed set on 'high' permanently. I had been prescribed beta-blockers by my GP, and had given up my four-day a week job because I was too unwell to do it. A local homeopath was recommended by my sister, and I went along. I had little faith in homeopathy, but this practitioner had also been a GP and psychiatrist before. She listened to me closely as I replied to her questions about my childhood and then recommended I find a transpersonal therapist, after I had told her about my early years.

'No one valued you as a child, and you're not valuing yourself now. I think if you did some work around the grief that you are carrying about your parents' deaths, you might find that it is enormously helpful. You may find you even have a change of career. I was recently on a weekend course with the Transpersonal Society, and I was amazed by how much psychotherapy has moved on since I was practising as a doctor years ago.'

The little white tablets she gave me (argent nitrate) helped the panic attacks to subside almost completely, which was wonderful, and following her advice I made some calls, found Jana, and two weeks later began the work that was to lead me to a new understanding about myself. Jana has done a lot of work with addicts too, so when our problems with Will started, I began talking to her about cannabis addiction as well as my own past. So, Jana knows our story, and has now met Guy twice.

This second time, Guy seemed very relaxed and peaceful, eager to talk, learning fast how to talk about feelings rather than the 'truth' of a situation. Jana later told me that she had found what he said very moving, and it was. He talked about how he felt about his mother and sister having allied themselves with Will against him. Jana asked him what the feeling was.

'I think the thing that I've always felt about my family is that they don't listen to what I have to say. That's always been the worst thing and it's still going on. I also feel that things go on behind my back, and I don't like it. There was some medical issue with my sister back in the eighties and I wasn't allowed to know what it was. Secrecy and not being listened to, those are the things that upset me most.

'Will has done some terrible things, including stealing whilst with my mother, indeed even stealing from her, and she doesn't want to see that, preferring to think badly of me and Deb than to see her grandchild blamed. She doesn't want to see things from my point of view, preferring to believe Will, when most of what he tells her is lies. It's bizarre and hurtful.'

Jana then explained about 'the shadow': that in relationships sometimes what is being dealt with are the 'shadows' of people who have been in our past – the witches and wizards of the past, usually our parents. When something triggers it, therefore, I can become to him his mother or his sister, and old behaviours and feelings come to the surface to be played out. Equally, she explained, it can happen for me, when he's being controlling or 'not very nice' as she put it, I will view him, at that moment, as my stepfather and behave and feel accordingly. This happens a lot with couples, she explained, but if you can become aware of this, you can stop it and place those shadows firmly to one side so that you can deal with each other again, the authentic person, in a place of light.

Interesting stuff. Jana went on to say that when we were talking to each other, we could try focusing on how we were feeling, and then express ourselves from that space. This would help, she said.

Guy said that he felt beatific afterwards.

'I've let go. Nothing bothers me any more, I'm in the flow. Whatever happens with Will, it's his life. I can do very little any more. A relationship based on lies is no relationship at all, so what's the point?'

We had been discussing strategies surrounding William, especially around his lying, which made us feel as if we were wasting our time having our checking-in meetings once a week.

We decided that we would like to back off completely from Will, and after our session with Jana, wrote to him to tell him that we wouldn't be meeting him again until the beginning of September, and that there was little point if at our meetings he was going to lie. We also told him that we were not prepared to foot the bill for any more rent or deposits for flats. His present house in Blackheath village has just been sold, and all the tenants have to leave by 14 September. I have begun to panic at the idea of him not having anywhere to live, yet know that allowing him to freefall is probably the only way of ensuring that things come to a head quickly. However, what seems to have happened before when we have tried this is that Will then phones me in a very distressed state, and my reaction has been to jump and try to help him. The pattern has been that he doesn't respond to the help I offer, and I end up feeling frazzled and hurt.

We discussed what to do in this situation and Jana said that with any pattern that is being built up – in this case Will trying to suck me in, to assuage his own painful feelings – it can be changed. It was agreed between the three of us that when Will calls I will tell him that I will call him back later – half an hour, an hour, whatever seems appropriate, but *later*, by which time his energy of urgently needing me will have changed.

I tried this and it helped, but it's hard and deeply confusing because one part of me wants to leap to his call and help him, so that he doesn't feel alone and upset, yet I know from past history that often when we do something nice for him, he almost immediately does something horrible. I can't help him through his addiction; only he can do that and he has to reach the point where he realizes that he needs to get help to stay off cannabis, and thereby regain his health and his life. Apparently, these strategies are the ones that work – setting very clear boundaries will help both us and him.

The plan seemed to be working. When Will phoned the next day asking to speak to me, Guy said I was busy. I phoned him back some hours later. He was confused, saying that he had nowhere to live, no money, no job, there was little of any good in his life.

'Your main problem is the cannabis, yet you can't see that. You need to get into rehab – for months this time – to really get off the stuff and then you can turn your life around. I know you can do it,' I began saying.

'Yeah, I know you think it's the cannabis, but it's more than that. I came off it before and still felt awful. I haven't smoked for a week now and I don't feel any better. I still hate myself for everything I've done. What I did to my girlfriend's family isn't going to go away because I get off cannabis. What if it's me and not weed, have you thought of that? I'll give up weed and I'll still have all my problems to face. I can't bear the thought of that.'

We talked for around an hour. As Will calmed down, and I began to say goodbye, Will said he knew how his father felt about him. 'I know,' he said, 'that Dad thinks I try to suck you in, so could you please not tell him what we've been talking about?' 'No, Will,' I replied, 'Guy and I are in this together. I don't keep things from him, but I won't go into details if that would help.'

The next time he called, he sounded much better, saying he'd got a job working as a 'charity mugger' on Oxford Street. I phoned him after his first day on the job, which was the next day and he said he was enjoying it. He phoned over the weekend to say that he really liked it.

'You know, I'm good at this. They are giving me a station to do and apparently they don't do that unless you're okay at it. I know you don't think it's a proper job, but I like talking to people. Standing outside Top Shop today was fun 'cos I was talking to all these buff young girls and they seem to like talking to me. We have a laugh.'

Phew. Relieved to hear joy in his voice, and enjoying having a conversation that was light and positive, I told him how good that was, that of course he would be a success, it was a proper job, he just had to focus now and stay off the weed.

'No, I'm not even thinking about smoking. Just enjoying a normal life, going home after work, putting a meal on – it's fine. Funny though, my supervisor was telling me that he used to do a lot of draw and it made his guts ache like crazy. He doesn't do it now.'

Will used to get painful stomach problems, which I knew must have been related to the vast quantities of draw he was doing, but never admitted by him. So, this was interesting. Not attaching to outcomes is so important for me, but I smiled and thought that meeting someone else who had not reacted well to weed had to be a good thing. The company he works for is called Evolution, he said, which also made me smile. He needs to evolve, and how!

At the end of our conversation, I said, 'Well done' to him, and he said, 'For what? I haven't done anything.' 'Just for doing what you're doing, focusing on what you need to do and getting yourself sorted out.' We also talked about how he was going to fund a new place to live. Will has some more money coming to him from another investment put in place for him by his grandparents, and I suggested he talk to his grandmother about having this money now.

'Yes,' he said, 'I'd like somewhere nice to live.'

We talked some more about this. I was trying to paint a picture of a life free from weed, living in a nice place, making new friends, moving on. He said that he understood how difficult it had been for us because he lies, and that he was determined to tell us the truth from now on. It was one of the best conversations we have had for some time.

The phone rang at half past three the next morning. I didn't answer it, but it woke me up and then I began wondering who it could have been. Going into the study next door, I checked the phone – a new message – from the custody officer at Charing Cross police station, saying that they have my son in custody and would I phone back to verify his address. What?! No name though. I thought it must have been Jack who had been out that night, and had still been out when we went to bed. Jack's bedroom door was closed, but with the phone still in my hand I went in and put the light on – oh, he was in bed. Right, so that means it must be Will. I felt better then. At least Jack was fine.

Will was in custody for disorderly conduct. He hadn't given our address, but his own (which was new), but would I confirm that it was correct? 'Disorderly conduct,' they said. Well, that's almost quaint to me – I'd started to sweat as I asked why they were holding him, concerned that the reply would be to do with theft or drugs. I couldn't get back to sleep again, though, and when Guy woke later I told him what had happened. He hadn't heard the phone. He grinned when I told him.

'Well, if you thought that material for the *Diaries* was going to dry up... !'

He phoned his mother the next day, asking if she wanted to meet for lunch, which she couldn't, and then mentioning that Will had been arrested the night before. He regretted doing this later.

'Very lower-self, I'm afraid,' he said to me later. 'I was doing it out of spite and now I feel awful. I was doing it for the wrong reasons. A truth told with bad intent and all that.'

Jack was there at the time, and turning to his father said, 'Maybe now she'll see what Will's like. What is it about him? She's always treated him like a prince – even when we were little she used to push me back when we were walking together and say "Give William his space". I don't get it, and she doesn't want to admit how badly wrong that boy's gone. Maybe now she'll have to. You did the right thing, Dad.'

I agreed with Jack. Guy smiled briefly, saying thanks to us both.

25 September

Plant attack

Will rang me yesterday. I hadn't heard from him for over a week. I'm getting stronger at dealing with his calls, not as jumpy, but I want this whole saga to end now. I'm tired of it all, and I want my son back. The campaign is going well, the website and the online *Diaries* have helped a lot of people, so you can stop now, William, you can come home and be part of our family again. You can be you again. I don't understand why all of this is taking so long. Come home and stop being an idiot. What happened? Why was our family torn apart? Oh, that's right – someone decided that cannabis was a soft drug, and that it was okay for children to take it. Who are these people? I guess 'it's society wot dunnit' – and society is made up of people – us. So, it's up to us to put it right, and to recognize that an elephant has indeed walked into the room; it's time we all noticed. Meanwhile…

William has told me this week that he is now living with friends. Homeless in other words. Oh, God.

'What happened to the flat that you had lined up?' I asked.

'Oh, nothing. The guy wasn't there and I've been looking all day for places and they are all horrible,' he said. 'I've been living with friends partly and partly at the Lucas.'

The Lucas is a local hotel. He had rung me on the day he was due to move out of the house he'd been living in since early summer. He had been told on the day he'd moved in there that it was a short-let only, that the house was being sold and that he would have to move out by the second week of September. Which was now. Three months' notice is enough, surely. Especially when he spent most of that time doing, well, nothing. He had rung on moving day to say that he had found a new place ('Really nice. It's all new, with wireless broadband and everything. The guy says I can have it.') but that he couldn't move in for a few days so what should he do?

Because Will had now been given the money from his grandparents' trust for him, I had recommended he find a hotel and stay there until he could move, which he said was in a couple of days. It seems that's what he has done.

'I've got a cheque for you though, and I've bought you a necklace to replace the other one – cost more than £250 – so I'll need to give it to you. I'm carrying all this around with me, with my bags and everything.'

Will was referring to what I had asked for at our last meeting, last weekend, when we had met for a pizza: Guy, Jack and myself. The necklace was a reference to the one he had stolen at his grandmother's eightieth party at our house two years ago.

I had insisted Will take me to where he had pawned my necklace. It was one of those places with a buzzer on the door, where large garish pieces of gold jewellery hang on headless plastic necks in the window. As you already know, it was too late to redeem my piece. It had been melted down for the gold, I was told. A shop assistant started to pick through what looked like gold filings on a large chopping board at the back. He found what he was looking for. I was offered the little red stone from the necklace, a small but thick piece of gold still on the back of it, bearing its hallmark. I couldn't bear to take it after what they'd done. It felt like I was being offered someone's internal organs after they had died.

'How much did he get for it?' I asked the man motioning over to Will. Could this really be happening to me? I'd waited weeks since I'd lost my jewellery, and had been toyed with by Will, in order to reach this moment. And I was too late.

'Twenty pounds,' he said.

'Didn't it occur to you that the necklace might have been stolen? That was mine, not his!' I said pointing over to Will again. He had turned away. 'What sort of outfit are you running here?'

I'd have slammed out of the shop but you have to wait until you are buzzed out. They lock you in as well as out.

Last weekend, Guy had a lot of work to do for the next day's case, and was looking stressed even before we left the house to go and meet Will. We had talked beforehand about how we should behave towards him – it had been over a month since we had seen him. Should we just listen to him, and not question him about his life – for example, what had happened subsequent to his arrest? It's hard to know what to do when past experience informs us that most of the things he tells us are lies. We want to believe what he says, and then it turns out to be a not-very-carefully-constructed fiction. 'How can you have a relationship with anyone based on lies?' we ask each other, most days, and the question hangs there looking for an answer, but not one that we can provide.

Our weekly meetings had ended, back in the summer, when we had decided to have a break from seeing him, you'll remember, after the last time when he stormed out. I hadn't been behaving well, either, deciding to confront him about the truth of what he was telling us.

Two days after we had been phoned in the early hours by Charing Cross police to say they had Will in custody, he rang me. I had been trying to ring him the day after it had happened, but his phone was switched off. I had rung my sister then, and told her about it. I was in Greenwich Park, with Lily playing around me, my phone looking up at me temptingly from the basket where I carry Lily's toys, lead and treats. I have become an organized puppy-mum. This puppy has almost saved my life, maybe. When I look at her, I smile, and we all start the day like that: smiling and talking about the naughty things that Lily does, sometimes one of us having to chase her into the garden as she disappears through the dog-flap with a soft leather shoe (not before she's made sure that we have seen her, of course). Jack was right when he said that she has given us all something to talk about (besides Will, I think he meant).

Sitting on a mound surrounded by trees I didn't know the names of, I dialled my sister's number, and began talking, a little manically, about what had happened to Will. She listened and then said:

'Well, you seem to be taking it very calmly. I mean – how do you do it? On and on the whole thing goes. What the hell is wrong with him? Why can't he get his life together? Oh, Debbie, I am sorry.'

I looked up towards the autumn sun and a surprisingly blue sky, and then down again to smile at Lily as she brought back the ball I'd thrown for her. Those were words I needed to hear. We are close now, but my relationship with my older sister was difficult when we were kids. She was bad-tempered and angry towards me often, and yet she also tried to take the place of our mother, to a certain extent, once Mum had died, when we were 16 and 12. I understand now where that anger came from. If I'd known then what I know now...

Our dad went out one day when my sister was six, and I was two. After putting on his hat in front of the mirror, he kissed us all and headed off to the local railway embankment. Climbing down it he lay with his head on the track, to wait for death. Neither of us was told he'd died, but we were informed by our mother, some months later, that we had a new daddy and that we were to forget about the other one, and call this one 'Daddy' now. Our surname was changed soon after. I promptly did as I was told; I would have done anything I was asked. So, emptying my mind of any memory of any other father, I accepted the stranger. My sister agreed too, but being so much older she remembered her father well; they had been close, and the buried memories acted like rocket fuel, exploding and burning their way up and out of her mouth whenever she was upset.

I understand her childhood pain, now, because it was the same pain I was carrying – I just had not been aware, before finding out about my father, of where it had come from. A double wound too, for both of us, because our mother then died, leaving us with the stranger, before she could tell us the truth about our early lives and who we really were. We both said recently that we think about her every day. But for me it's now pain mixed with joy, because I've learnt to recall, without flinching, the happy times we had together and be glad that such a loving, sunny woman had once been my mum.

When William finally rang me, he sounded genuinely contrite.

'I'm so sorry the police had to ring you. They needed to verify my address – and I gave them my flatmate's number but he wasn't picking up. I was with Jake, who was arrested for having fake ID, even though he is 18 now. Yeah, I got really cross with the police for taking him away and threw my bottle of water at the van, so they put the cuffs on me too. They let me go, though, a few hours later, so there's no harm done. I can't believe it's happened to me again. I thought last time would be the last time, really.'

So, a reasonable explanation I suppose. Guy didn't think it added up to much of a story, and thought it unlikely that the police would bother arresting someone for such a thing. I was chatting to a friend later that week and she said that sniffer-dogs were being used at the London stations these days, and that her son had been arrested in the summer for possession of two ecstasy tablets. This was probably more like the truth. Will's friend, Jake, is a habitual cannabis smoker – he used to go to the same crammer as Will and each time that we had met him, he had looked and acted very stoned.

Will went on to say that he was still working, as a charity name-finder in the West End, and I believed him. He sounded upbeat and happy, if not tired. He told me he was working the next day, and for five days after that – that was his shift that week. However, as I was driving through the village the next day, I saw him cross the road, teeth sinking deep into a Gregg's meat pie, with another one of his cannabis friends from his ex-college. I beeped the horn to let him know I'd seen him. 'Gotcha,' I thought, and then, aware that my heart rate had suddenly gone up, realized how angry I was to have been lied to (again). Had the job ever existed?

I know he wants me to think well of him. He told me that recently on the phone – no matter what happens everyone wants the approval of their mum. Right, but a funny way of going about it.

Our meeting with him last week, in the pizzeria, was strained. Jana, our counsellor, had advised us that instead of getting angry about the lies he was telling, to look on his 'stories' as if we were observing a film. Detachment – not getting drawn in. His reality versus our reality. Easy! I think even the Dalai Lama would find Will a challenge.

During our meal with Will, Guy sat there saying little, looking very uncomfortable, arms crossed. Jack and Will chatted together happily about music and films. Alex was not there, choosing to stay at home.

Will said he was working and hoping to move into his new flat soon. When the bill came, I looked at Will and asked if he wanted to treat us now he had money. He had no money on him he said. Of course not. I asked then if he was going to replace the necklace that he had stolen from me and sold last year. Oh, and what about reimbursing the money he'd stolen from us in the form of cheques and cash?

'I do think about what I've done, you know. I have got a conscience. I'd forgotten about the necklace... .'

'Yes, well, I haven't,' I said.' Daddy bought me that, a unique piece that cost over £200 and you got twenty quid for it after it was melted down. I'd like a replacement or the money, please. I can't believe you come out without any money; you've got more money than I've got now. I can't remember when you've ever bought me as much as a cup of coffee, ever!'

I looked over at Jack and Guy. Both were silent, sitting back in their chairs. I smiled at Jack and he shrugged and looked away. Guy said nothing, which I don't think I'd ever seen before. What was going on? I was suddenly on my own. I'd ruined the evening for Jack, and he so rarely sees his brother, I began thinking. But as we walked out of the restaurant, I thought differently. No, Will needs telling. He's living in a hotel. We've been through so much, why shouldn't he pay some of it back?

'You can start putting things right now, William, now you have some money,' I said, as we stood outside ready to part. 'People forget very quickly, you know. Most people don't hold grudges for long, you'll see.'

'Okay, well, a grand should cover it, shouldn't it? I'll send you a cheque.'

He turned and walked away then. Jack began telling his father that he wouldn't be coming out with us and Will again.

'I'll meet him on my own. I hate it when Mum has a go at him. It's not fair on the rest of us. She didn't have to do that; it was awful.'

A week later, and William appears to be homeless. It's pointless us getting involved in trying to find him somewhere to live. We've done that and it always ends badly. He has to do this on his own, and he can do it. He rang again yesterday to say he was bringing over the cheque and necklace and that he'd decided to go away for a while.

'It's just an idea. I'm ringing to let you know I'm going away. A mate of mine's dad is opening a bar in Spain, so I may go over there with him. Just to let you know. I can't stand another autumn here, on my own again for my birthday and Christmas in some grotty room. I can't do this any more. My life's going nowhere. I've got to do something.'

I said it was a good idea to get away, and where in Spain? He didn't know.

'Nothing's concrete yet'.

He still rings, and always wants to talk to me. I love him so much and want him back, but as a credible human being, not as someone I can't trust.

A few weeks ago I was sitting clutching another mug of tea in front of the little bookcase in our kitchen. On top of it is the Lily-stone still, and also are family photos from my childhood, and ones of Guy and all three boys too. When I was doing my bereavement work with Jana she recommended I get out photos of my parents, light a candle there and just sit and think about them, letting the feelings come. The idea was to bring my parents back into my life before I could start to say goodbye to them. As I sat there now, years on, I began to look at a photo of William that I had placed there recently. He is in school uniform, at the same kitchen table I'm sitting close to now, blowing out candles on his birthday – there are seven of them. I thought how wonderful he looks and I smiled. At the bottom of the bookcase, my eye was caught by a book I don't think anyone has ever read. It was a children's slim picture book, possibly a school reading book – *Plant Attack* was the title. I couldn't remember where it had come from. Picking it up, I turned it over and on the back read that 'this book is about a plant that seems harmless, but is in fact highly dangerous and tries to kill two young brothers'.

As I turned to the middle of the book, there was a drawing of a child who looked incredibly like William in the photo I had just been looking at – same haircut, same age. He had the huge plant tendrils around his neck and was losing consciousness, falling to the ground in a coma-like state. The blurb on the back of the book explained it all. 'It looks quite harmless at first, but this is no ordinary plant. It seems to move on its own and Adam has this eerie feeling that the plant is trying to strangle him. That night he and his brother awake to find it hanging from the ceiling. Then the plant starts to grow, its tendrils creeping nearer, wrapping around his arms, touching his hair. Before they know it, they are trapped.'

A month before I had broken down crying, huge racking sobs. I hadn't cried like that for years, but it had hit me that William was lost to us, and the pain was intense. Alex was downstairs watching TV, everyone else was out. I was sitting in the corridor outside Will's old room, under a framed sampler that had been sewn for him when he was born. My legs were pulled up under my chin, my head in my hands. Alex heard me and came running up the stairs. He sat down beside me, and putting his arms around me began telling me that the William we all remember has gone, he was no longer in that body, almost as though William had been replaced by some huge weed, he said. I listened and it helped me, because if I could stop thinking of the person I now knew as not my beautiful son, but as something that had taken him over, then maybe I could cope better.

Now, sitting here in the kitchen a month or so later, I seemed to be being shown the same thing that Alex had told me. A plant that is more dangerous than first thought of. I'm sure the seven-year-old Will would have never predicted that he would be attacked by such a thing. He would have laughed and said that was impossible. Weed: it got a hold of him and he has lain in a coma ever since.

15 October

I used to care but things have changed

I haven't seen or heard from William for over a week. He texted me last Saturday evening to ask if I still didn't want to hear from him. I could hear my phone buzz in my pocket, as the text came in. Guy and I were walking to Greenwich Theatre to see a new play by a local writer, Blake Morrison, with whom Guy occasionally plays tennis. Tickets had been bought months before by a friend; a large group of us were meeting. Both of us were unenthusiastic about going out; I had been lacking in energy for days, and had slept for a couple of hours that afternoon. But I had showered, changed, straightened my normally curly hair (which always makes me feel better and more like someone from this decade), and then in minutes created an outfit out of a red mini-dress from last year, black tights and recently acquired black high-heeled boots. I was now feeling wonderful. Looking down at the worn centuries-old paving stones as we walked down Crooms Hill, the adjacent park's chestnut fragrance in the air, I took out my phone and read the message from Will. I began to reply then cancelled it. What was the point? What would I say?

The restaurant encounter when I had confronted William and upset Jack had been two weeks before. He had rung several times since then to say that he had a cheque and a necklace to give us (well, the necklace was for me obviously). He had promised when we had parted the week previously that he would do this, at my suggestion, and I hoped now that what he said he really meant. He had sounded genuine when he called, but my way of listening to what he says on the phone is to do just that, listen and say very little. The only way not to get hurt is by not attaching any emotion to contact with him. Still unsure how you do this, but I give it a try every time. On the phone I listened to his news: he said he still didn't have anywhere to live, he just couldn't find a place he liked, and anyway he didn't want to commit to another six months when he almost certainly would go abroad. He told me again that he didn't want to be in London for his birthday and then for Christmas, alone, and how depressing that would be. He was still working for the charity fund-raisers, every day, he said. I didn't believe it. Jack and I had both seen him in the middle of the day on separate occasions, each time with one of his cannabis friends.

'I'm staying at Jake's and in hotels too. I'm working every day and carrying around this necklace that's worth over £250 and a cheque for a grand, so I need to meet you and give them to you. It's crazy me carrying this stuff around with me.'

You'll remember that Jake was the friend I'd seen him with in Blackheath when he was supposed to be working, whom he had met whilst at the Kensington crammer, having a third attempt at ASs. I felt a physical pain in my stomach, an acidic mix of shame and incredulity, when Will said these things: my own adored son staying with another person's family when he's nearly twenty? Please let this not be happening. But it is, and I can't seem to do a thing about it. A nightmare you don't wake up from. If I'd known this when William was little...what would I have thought? My sunny, handsome, clever little boy who loved people and was so sociable. Drug addiction was what happened to poor, uneducated people who knew no better, not to people from caring families with everything to live for. Wasn't it? Someone help me here. But things have changed now, there is skunk in schools and it's accepted as part of the youth culture. Some come unstuck, like Will, as he heads towards psychosis yet remains unconvinced of cannabis' dangers, confused because 'everyone' is doing it. The Government have virtually decriminalized it, not everyone gets ill, and it's just a bit of puff that you can stop doing any time. Isn't it?

You'll recall that Jake had looked stoned every time I'd seen him, though that was some time ago now. This was another reason I didn't believe Will was working – how could he be if he was staying at a friend's and effectively homeless? Logistically that was impossible. He couldn't get to one hour a week at college when he was living with us or with his grandma, when everything was organized for him. This was all a fiction, but he did sound convincing, and I told myself again that paying us back for money and belongings he had stolen was a good way for him to begin to put things right, now he had funds.

Our Action Group had met earlier this week, and arriving home afterwards I was told by Jack that William had rung to say that he was moving into a new flat the next day, and needed to give me both money and necklace. Kicking off my shoes in the hallway, as Jack's disembodied voice told me this from upstairs, I headed into the kitchen, making my way to the kettle via an excited Lily, who is always so glad to see me. She is now seven months old, and gorgeous. I remember years ago asking a friend who had just bought a small, white, fluffy dog how she was getting on with him, and she said that now her children were teenagers, and sometimes grumpy when they came home, how nice it was to be greeted enthusiastically by her dog every time. Now I know what she means.

William rang soon after, as I was hugging a tea cup in the hallway and throwing a ball for Lily to bound and slide after. I arranged to meet him in a couple of days' time, at a restaurant in the village. He wanted to give me what he had, so let's do that I said. If Guy or Jack are around, I told him, they will come along too; otherwise it will be just me.

As it turned out, Guy was out of London on the day we planned to meet, and Jack said that he didn't want to come after last time. So, feeling happy at the thought of seeing William again, I quickly made a meal for Alex and Jack, and went upstairs to get changed. William was in my thoughts; I was wondering how he was and how the meeting would go, what I should expect, what I should say and not say (hang on, this is my son I'm meeting, not some stranger – really?) The phone rang; I heard Jack answer. It was William wanting to talk to me.

'I'm still in Victoria. I won't be able to get there by seven, not for another hour or so. And I don't have the cheque or the necklace. They're at Jake's, and no one's going to be there until later. They're all out and won't be back for ages. Do you want to cancel, then?'

'No, I'm ready to come out,' I said, quietly.

'What's the matter? You sound strange. Have you been crying? Are you mad with me, because if you are I'd rather not meet? I can't stand another argument.'

'What? I'm fine. I'd planned to come out, so let's meet. I can take you back to where you're staying afterwards and we can pick up the stuff there,' I said, with no hint of sarcasm.

This all seemed straightforward, although I knew what Guy would have said. But Guy wasn't there, and I was in the mood for a large glass of red wine in our local Café Rouge. It was raining outside and it would be cosy in there.

'Well, that might not be till very late. They're out celebrating a birthday, and won't be back till around 10.30 or so.'

'That's fine. It doesn't matter. We can do that. I'm okay.'

'Fine. Well, I'll pay for the meal. How's that?'

Oh, an improvement on last time. Maybe we are getting through after all. But I wasn't going to see either a necklace or a cheque tonight, and knew that I should have postponed the meeting, but I didn't.

Guy and I had been to have another counselling session with Jana the previous week. We had talked about our lives without William, what we might expect, what we might do to help ourselves and, by extension, him. Jana had been saying for some time that William will continue with 'hysterical' behaviour, as she put it, because it serves his need to make sure he can draw us (or, rather, me) in. By hysterical she meant whipping up some emotional situation that requires a response from us. He will need to be in control, she said; that will be important to him, so that he can feel he retains power in the relationship. She told us that often addicts operate from the polarities of victim or aggressor. We both recognized that pattern in William.

'But, won't he get bored of doing this eventually? Why would anyone want to keep repeating the same behaviour, when it doesn't go anywhere? I don't understand what he gets out of it,' I asked.

Jana explained that he wouldn't get bored. We can help him by not getting drawn into the 'games' that he tries to play, which are most successful with me. As long as he's getting a reaction, that's feeding him.

'There will be situations that he will create so he can pull you back into his life, so he knows he has you there. I don't think he's ready to make any big changes in his life at the moment; it's long term with him. Sometimes addicts will see a friend die, or get very ill from drugs, and maybe then they will seek a change, but sometimes not even then. We don't know what it will be with William, what will make him look to change. With change, people are either in such pain that they have to move on or they are attracted by such an exciting, bright, different position that they move towards it and make the change that way. It's either one or the other, and we don't know at the moment what it is that will make William move from the position he's in. People talk about "rockbottom", but that's different for everyone.'

So, I had been warned about the potential games that William would continue to play with me, yet here I was agreeing to meet him. He had sounded as if he really wanted to off-load the money and jewellery, and yet here we were weeks on and he still hadn't handed over either. Never mind. I wanted to see him, and began to feel a surge of something like excitement at the prospect of seeing him again.

He was late arriving. I had already ordered my glass of red wine and was trying to find something on the menu I could eat. Why are there never enough vegetarian options? I refuse to have yet another ubiquitous goat's cheese salad with caramelised onions. Guess I'm lucky when there is anything at all: friends of ours have recently opened a new restaurant in London, and are almost proud that there are no veggie options on the menu at all. Hmm, curious.

William came in looking pale with grey shadows under his eyes, but his hair was clean and freshly cut (he'd finally been for the much talked about hair-cut it would appear). His clothes looked grubby though and smelt of smoke. I had brought a bag of clothes he'd been talking about, that were still at our house; they had been washed and ironed. He seemed pleased and smiled as he sat down heavily opposite me. I was irritated when he said he didn't want to eat anything. I must have looked disappointed, because he then grudgingly ordered two starters. We talked, but there was no depth. Most of what he said I knew was not the truth.

He was still working, had been doing so today, and was knackered. I began to sense he was uncomfortable; he was looking away from me most of the time. I always feel I want to talk either about what he's doing (but the replies never sound like the truth) or about his future plans, which are always the same but never move from the thoughts stage. He said he wasn't doing any cannabis. I thought this unlikely as Jake was a cannabis friend, and said so: he was the one he'd been with when they were both arrested.

'Yeah, well, how do you know? He used to do weed but not anymore.'

'So, his parents are okay with you staying there?'

'Yes, they love me.'

Right. I said I'd take him back there and we'd get the things, as we'd agreed. He got up then, saying that he didn't know where he was staying that night, and didn't want to go back to Jake's because they might be getting fed up with him. Picking up the bag I had brought, he walked out of the restaurant. My first raging thoughts were about the bill. He has thousands in the bank now and I'm yet again picking up the tab. He's still not honouring his promises.

I ordered coffee and the bill, and sat there wanting to scream. I'd brought along the book I was in the middle of, and read a page to calm myself a little, then paid and left the restaurant.

As I was walking back to my car, which I'd parked by the church at the top of the village, I saw William coming down the hill, smiling at a piece of paper or card that he was holding. It looked like he had just checked into the Lucas Hotel, which was located a short distance away, and he was holding a key card.

He saw me and called out, 'Sorry', crossing over the road towards me.

I started shouting as he approached.

'You walk out leaving me in the middle of a restaurant by myself. You said you'd pay the bill, and you didn't – what sort of person have you turned into? Just stay away from me. I can't do this any more!'

'I'll pay then,' he said putting his hand towards the pocket of his jeans.

'Yeah, alright then. £25 is what I paid. That would be very nice. I

157

haven't got the other things you said you'd bring, but that would be a good start I suppose,' I said, really getting angry now. God, how did things get this bad? An old refrain, but a familiar one.

'Oh, but I need all my money,' he said.

'Oh really? Well I can tell you, I've had enough of your silly games – I want you out of my life!! Why don't you just fuck off!!'

I turned to cross the road, and an oncoming car stopped with screeching brakes just in time for me not to go under its wheels.

(Okay, just take your time. There's no need to get yourself killed.)

I waited for a gap in the traffic and headed across to the other side, not looking back. Rain was really coming down now, just to reflect my mood. As I drove off too fast, I saw Will coming back up the other way as if he was trying to find me. He looked solemn.

I didn't start crying until I got home. Guy had already gone to bed, which I took to be another strand of the abandonment tapestry that was being woven around me that night.

My phone started to ring. It was Will again.

'Look, I'm sorry about tonight. I'll post the necklace through the door.'

'Don't bother. I don't want to hear from you again. I used to care but things have changed,' I shouted, and flapped the phone shut. That last line was the title of a Bob Dylan song that Guy and I like, and both feel it describes how we feel about our son these days.

Jack came down from upstairs and asked me if I was okay and how was it with Will? I'd gone into the sitting room, after cuddling and playing with Lily for a while. Jack sat down next to me on the sofa, looking concerned.

'Oh, you won't believe it, Jack. I'm really worried this time, though, that he's becoming irrational. Why meet me tonight, just to upset me? I don't think he had any intention of honouring his promises to give me a necklace. He told me it was turquoise, details about it. I don't think it exists.'

Will texted then to say that he would drop off the necklace and that he loved me. I texted him back to say that my son had died a long time ago, to be replaced by a weed, and that he should now leave me to mourn in peace. A bit dramatic, maybe, but it helped me to put that in writing to him, because I need to remember that this stranger may look like my son, but acts nothing like him. He has changed dramatically through addiction; whether he will ever be as I remember I don't know.

26 November

Happy families

The conference on 'Cannabis and Children' which was held in the House of Commons on 30 October went very well. Mary Brett and I had worked on little else for weeks before, and it's so true that everything is in the planning. Alex had agreed to be one of the speakers, and talked about his experience of being affected by a brother's addiction. Many of us had tears in our eyes at that point. It was wonderful to meet so many other parents there, some of whom I had only been in email contact with before. A group of us walked down to 10 Downing Street afterwards to deliver our petition, which had been signed on our website by hundreds.

Our family's situation does not get better, except that Jack and Alex are fine. I am, however, wondering about moving Alex from his present school. His fear that he might turn out the way William has, and that being at the same school is going to make that more likely, has continued. Despite our talks with him, he says he still does not feel safe there, so maybe it's time for a change. Guy is still in a very good space, and so is Jack.

Since the conference though, I have not felt great – I've had severe pain in my lower back, and have been forced to rest and seek out help from an osteopath, which may be working; I certainly feel slightly better today, though still weary and jumpy. We have had a couple of turbulent days, though, so that's not surprising. Both William's and Guy's birthdays are this week – Guy's on Thursday and Will's on Saturday. Having had no contact with William for some weeks now, not since I wrote the last *Diary* entry, I was half-expecting that Will would begin to contact me as his birthday draws nearer. His birthday has always been important to him. A text from him at the weekend asked me to ring if I could (please).

We were all eating supper in the kitchen last Saturday evening as my phone buzzed the message's arrival. Guy looked over at me, thoughtfully, as I read the message out, and said: 'Evelyn Waugh once said, "If someone wants to get in touch with me – if it's important – let them write me a letter".'

He had such a funny expression on his face, as he was recalling this, that I found myself laughing loudly.

'Yes, that would be nice,' I said, and decided not to respond to Will's text. Yes, I would await a letter.

Will had promised us just that, of course, some weeks ago (about six I think). A cheque would be sent to us, he said. ('Would a thousand do?' I remember the words vividly.)

Then there were the various telephone calls saying he was carrying around both a necklace and a cheque to give me.

And the promise he made to bring the necklace round when I did meet him for supper weeks later. No missive has been delivered subsequently by Royal Mail either.

The day before the conference at Westminster, which was probably one of the busiest in my life, I got a call from William. I was sitting at my computer in my attic-room study, scanning emails, fielding scores of calls, and trying not to give in to the fear that had been trying to paralyze me since the weekend at the very thought of what I had let myself in for with the event. (Just whose idea was this anyway?) When the phone rang, I was hoping it was GMTV firming up their invitation for me to be on the sofa with Lorraine Kelly the next morning. I was dismayed to hear Will's voice. 'Hello, Mum, it's me.'

On one of my busiest days after weeks of silence? I was that morning working on getting as much publicity as possible. Our secretary, Lynne, had decided to take matters into her own hands after we had been let down by a (famous) PR-guru contact, who had said he'd write a press release for us and then seemed to enter some black hole. She'd penned one herself and emailed it to many, and we were now getting lots of calls; also calling were delegates anxious to have questions answered. And now here was Will.

'I'm at Grandma's.' I could hear my mother-in-law's voice in the background saying something to him.

'I'm not sure why I'm phoning. I know that the last time you told me you didn't want to see me again and told me to fuck off, in the village.'

Oh, nice, in front of the aged relation who hates swearing.

'Yeah, well I'm still waiting for the necklace and the money,' I snarled, feeling that familiar trapped sensation, as I prepared to be played with like a mouse by a cat.

'Well, I've got them here but my flat's been flooded and I'm down here staying with Grandma until I can get another place.'

'Well, look, I'm up to my eyes in it here. I'll call you back when I've got a minute.' I put the phone down angrily. More likely is that friends' parents have got sick of him staying and he has to disappear for a couple of days.

The phone rang again almost immediately.

The voice on the other end sounded like the Queen. I didn't think she'd been sent a press release. Oh, no, it wasn't her, just my mother-in-law in posh 'I'm going to give you a piece of my mind, so I've put on my best cut-glass accent' mode.

'Debra, it's me.' She sounded angry.

Oh, God, I could feel she was going to mention the fuck-off incident. Good mothers don't swear at their offspring. I knew I wasn't good enough for the job. I was suddenly transported back to my days as a 12-year-old girl, in a new school, whose mother was dying in a huge local hospital, yet noone was talking about it, being singled out by the headmistress for not having the right indoor shoes on. (*Please just leave me alone. I'm trying to fit in and know I don't.*)

'Look,' I said, 'I'm really up against it just now. We have our meeting in Parliament tomorrow. We're launching our campaign to try and help the next generation. I can't talk to you. I'll call you back.' I'd almost stopped breathing. All these years of doing yoga and meditation and I seem spectacularly useless at any form of adequate breathing techniques in the face of supreme stress.

The phone rang again. I let the machine get it. A message from Grandma this time.

'I'm very worried about William. He's really ill. Please phone me back.'

So, I phoned back 10 minutes later, unable to concentrate on anything else.

'I'm so worried about William. He's so ill. His place has been flooded and everything is ruined. It's so sad for him.'

'Do you believe him?'

'Yes, I do. I think we need to help him,' she said with a yodel in her voice. 'You are his mother, after all; it's all very well helping other people like you say you're doing but what about Will's future? Who's going to sort that out is what I want to know. You are his mother, you know!'

Please let me cope well with this and not lose my grip.

'Do you think he's got a future, then?' I said wanting to cry.

I know I'm his mother, I wanted to scream. This is not fair. I've tried to be a mother to him and every time I get screwed over. I don't feel I can defend myself though, especially from other people's mothers, hence the desire to cry. Whenever I've tried in the past my words have seemed to evaporate as I speak.

'Look, things are really impossible here. I'm so busy. I can't speak to you today. Give me till Wednesday when things are quieter and I'll call you back then.'

The phone rang again. It must be GMTV this time, I thought.

Will again. I could hear Grandma whispering in the background.

'I'm not sure what I'm supposed to be ringing about.'

I could hear 'tell her about...,' and then Will obviously getting cross with his grandmother hovering when he's on the phone.

I spoke instead.

'Look, William, you know I love you, don't you? But it's time you started to keep your promises, and fulfill what you've said you're going to do. That's important. You said you'd give me a necklace and the cheque, so where are they? I'll call you on Wednesday. Maybe we can do something then.'

Wednesday came and I didn't phone. Lack of courage, I suppose. I was also exhausted and wanted a day to myself.

We had, the four of us, some months before, discussed what we would do at Christmas. For years we have been taking it in turns to host Christmas. Last year was my sister's turn. It had not been an easy day, as you know, because Will wasn't living with us. This year the night-mare has closed in – we don't know where William is living. We could ask him, but what he says would probably be a lie, so what's the point? We're all so tired of this not-so-merry-go-round that we have given up hope of there being a happy conclusion for years. Alex's view is 'Good riddance, after all the problems he's caused this family. Let him go; I'm not interested any more.' Jack is too busy with A levels, his band, his friends and *My Space* (not in that order!).

As a family though, we had agreed some months before that we would have Christmas Day with just us (and little Lily this year, of course). Guy suggested that we have a meal with his family, and William, in a restaurant in London, the week before and whoever wanted to go could do so. He would also meet William for a drink on Christmas Day with whichever of us wanted to go. Alex said that he didn't want to see William at all for the moment, and so he wouldn't go. The rest of us would do so.

The restaurant has not been booked. After my last meeting with Wil-liam there seems little point. I can't bring myself to see him again – more lies to cope with. Guy has been wondering what to do – whether to go ahead and book something and invite his mum and sister or wait for them to talk to him about Christmas. No one is saying anything as a result.

But, Guy's mother rang on Sunday night, and left a message saying she was very worried about William and would we call her.

I could hear Guy talking to his mother, beginning with the 'How are you?' It seems she had been with Will last Saturday. She had gone up to London to meet him with a bag of clean clothes, things he'd left at her house the week before. She'd done that to save him the trip down to her house. I could hear Guy asking her why she was running around after him. Then he began to say that if William was ill he should go to a doctor, or to a hospital. A few more minutes of this, and he then went on to tell her that if she is worried about William she is going to have to keep her worries to herself because we are distanced from him now and intend to keep it that way; he is no longer our responsibility.

'I've got two other children here, who I am doing my best to nurture. That young man has made his decisions about his own pathway and until he turns his life around I will not get involved with him any more. The last time Deb met him he told her he had gifts and then didn't turn up with them. We can't keep going on like this; it's too hard. If you feel we are being too harsh, just read his last college report. You have a copy of it, from just a year ago. Those were the damning things that his teachers were saying about him, people who had only just met him. We fought hard for him not to be expelled from there, and he couldn't even be bothered to turn up for the one morning a week that we negotiated so he could get some basic AS levels. But you don't remember any of this, and you refuse to read those comments. You say he's ill? Well, I'm not surprised. Are you? He's abused his body so much. A lot of these kids end up committing suicide. He's a drug addict, Mum, and you've got to start accepting that. He will never come into this house again. We've tried everything and we're not going to do it any more.

'I have my memories of the son who was mine. I've got photos here to remind me. What Will has become is not my son. I have two other children who need my attention and I'm going to do my utmost to make sure their childhoods aren't ruined by what's happened here. But I will not have you ring me up and talk to me about Will and say how concerned you are. You've got to stop doing that. I don't want to hear about it.'

Firm, solid stuff, but also deeply upsetting.

William rang me the next day to ask if I wanted to meet him.

'No, I don't,' I said. 'Funny how you ring me now it's going to be your birthday at the end of the week.'

'Well, it's just that I haven't seen you for ages. I know I've been the world's worst son and all that – but I'm not doing a lot of the things I used to do. I'm getting my life back together. It's not easy when your family don't want to see you. I wanted to apologize. I don't want anything from you.'

'Well, I'd like something from you,' I said, becoming the hardened me that seems to come out now whenever I talk to him. 'I'd like the necklace, which I know you never bought, and I'd like the cheque you promised us.'

'I did have the necklace,' he started to say, 'but it was in a JD bag with other things and I was in a pub and it was stolen.'

I begin to laugh. The merry-go-round is starting up again – roll up, roll up. Not this time. Are you kidding?

'You know what? You are so full of rubbish. Do you think I'm stupid? I don't believe a word you say. And where's the cheque you said you had – you can send that through the post can't you?'

'Oh, well, I haven't got a cheque book,' he said.

'Right, well, I tell you what, William, why don't you just go away and leave me alone? I don't recognize you or anything you say – the son I had would not have spoken like this. Just leave me alone.'

With that I slammed the phone down.

Guy's mother was phoning at the same time as I was speaking to William and left a message. She sounded tearful and said it was quite urgent. I didn't return her call. More messages followed. She then rang my mobile.

I rang her back a couple of hours later, hoping by this time that she would be calmer.

The gist of her call was that we should have Will back to live with us.

'I think you're going to have to, darling. It's the only kind thing to do, the Christian thing you know. He can't cope on his own. He loves all of you, misses the boys dreadfully. He's got no one to do his washing. It's awful. I'm so worried it's breaking my heart. You've got to have him back with you. He should be with his family.'

I asked her what her vision was of his coming back here to live – and as I did so I remembered this time last year when she had told me that he should come back to live with us, and we took him back. He then spent most of his time lying in bed, smoking dope day and night, watching television. Within 24 hours of him being back we had found stolen property in his room, and the police had been called. Later we found that he'd written himself cheques on our account within a day of arriving too.

'Oh, he's different now. He's changed. He knows he needs to get A levels, and says there's a college in London where he can do evening classes, but he needs his family's support. You need to have him back to live with you.'

'Are you insane?' I asked. 'I've got two other kids here who I'm trying to bring up. He will never come back here to live.'

'Oh, Debra, how can you say that when you're his mother? It breaks my heart.'

The conversation went on for some time. I mentioned the promises Will had made, and had broken, and she began to say she had a cheque-book at her house. What? She just doesn't get it – it's not the money that's the issue.

I told her I was too upset to keep talking to her and would have to ring off.

When Guy came home, he rang her.

'I won't have you ringing up my family and upsetting them. I told you yesterday not to ring here and talk about William and the very next day you're doing so. Do you understand me when I say he will never live here again? Do you? Just answer the question. Do you understand that I mean that? Good. You are meddling and it's got to stop.'

I do understand that Guy's mother wants to put things right, and of course at birthday and Christmas-times she wants us to be a happy family again, but it doesn't work like that with drug addiction.

I feel I've been beaten up – twice. It's very hard for anyone to understand teenage addiction and what it can do to families unless you've experienced it yourself. It's also very confusing for the older generation to cope with, of course. It must seem so simple and logical: young people need the support of their families, yet in our case we can no longer offer that. We've tried to help him, sorting out accommodation, paying off debts and frauds to prevent him being prosecuted, you name it... We have tried to protect him, but each time he goes and does something else, so we have to give up. It can't be good for him either, being constantly bailed out. This way he has a chance of sorting out his future, if his scrambled brain will allow it.

Maybe in the future, possibly ten years from now – we can be a family again. But this being who was once our sunny, handsome, ambitious boy will have to take responsibility for his actions and make the changes, and be able to demonstrate that fully to us, because without that we could never trust him even to enter our house again.

24 December

A circle is completed

Looking back to when I started these *Diaries*, exactly a year ago, I can see the huge changes that we have made to our family situation, yet also how much work it has been. Making the recent decision to step right back from Will has been long in coming, but I know that it is the right one for us, and for him. It still hurts though, and I can't quite believe that we have had to do this. It is Christmas Eve; I began the *Diaries* exactly this time last year; a circle has been completed. As I re-read that first entry I am struck by how few glimpses there are of the optimism that I used once to have when our son first began smoking cannabis. I spent most of those preceding years, before beginning to write the *Diaries*, genuinely believing that we could have a new beginning, and keep our family together. Anything else was unthinkable. Even though at times I doubted my husband could do so, I was willing to forget the past, to forgive William, to begin again – so many times I announced to everyone that we were going to do this, each time looking over at William and seeing him nod and say that was what he wanted too. Then I began to give up, and it happened a year ago.

Living life in a house which we had had to convert into a fortress was unworkable. It was impossible, and exhausting, to police it all, to try to keep it a drug-free and smoke-free zone. We were constantly gearing up for the next time we would have to be strong about some infringement, a bit like trying to run a rehab unit. Our family life had become a living nightmare, and the underlying feeling that we were on our own with it all was becoming more than we could bear. Even our own families did not understand what was happening to us.

As I've explained before, on Christmas Day each year we take it in turns to host lunch – us, Guy's older sister, and my older sister. Both of our sisters are married with one son each, now 16 and 22. Three years ago, when Will had just turned 17, I went to my sister's house for the celebrations with my hand in tight bandages and a sling. Guy's sister and brother-in-law seemed not to notice, and didn't ask me about it. I was wounded by their lack of concern. Guy's mother had been shocked, but assured me that William had explained everything to her, and that my injuries had been the result of an accident. She was upset that William had not bought me anything to recompense for this, and told him off on Christmas Day for not putting this right, for which I was grateful. But she still maintained that it had been an accident. Guy explained the legal position to both Will and his mother. It had not been an accident, but assault. I mentioned this incident early on in the *Diaries* but what had really happened was that William had flown into a rage a week before Christmas, and begun trashing the house when I refused to give him the allowance we had agreed on (with the proviso that he must go to college each day). He had lain in bed for the previous days, stoned and refusing to go, so I told him that his allowance for that week was suspended. When I had tried to leave the house to get away from him he raged after me, slamming the heavy Victorian door on me as I passed through it, catching my hand. It was only when I was sitting in the car, planning to drive away, that I realised that my right index finger was badly split and oozing blood, and my hand severely bruised. Looking down at the steering wheel I could see large red drops forming on the hard plastic.

Our next-door neighbour, a New York banker, was on the street as this was all happening. As I walked down the pathway after the door had been slammed on me, he asked me if I was alright. 'Fine,' I said. (What was I saying? But I couldn't tell him what was happening, or ask for help, because I was so ashamed. After all, this is a nice neighbourhood. That man was something big in banking, and everyone knew that he had recently paid over a million quid for his house.) Holding my bleeding hand up to stop it dripping, I wondered what my new neighbour made of all of this, and then, looking up, saw William sit down heavily, arms crossed, on the car bonnet in front of me.

Curiously, my sister-in-law had rung in the middle of it all too. William had breathlessly answered the phone, as it rang in the hallway, panting due to his rage.

'Oh, hi, Martha. Yes, we're fine. Really? Great. Yes, okay. Thanks then, sure. Bye.' He was smiling, trying to catch his breath and had even laughed at something she had said, really polite. (She later said that she thought she had phoned in the middle of an orgy, presumably because of Will's breathlessness.)

Martha was calling. The phone. Maybe I should call the police, but not on your own son; that was impossible. William had sounded almost normal then, as he talked to his aunt. Surely he would stop now. But he didn't. As he replaced the receiver he began again – swiping more things from the hallway tables. I retreated into our front room, closing the door heavily behind me, and prayed that he would calm down. I could hear Jack, who was then 14, talking to William.

'Hey, just calm down. What are you doing? Stop it! Leave Mum alone. She's my mum too. Leave her alone. What's the matter with you? Stop it!'

William forced open the door to the front room, pushing hard; I was behind it trying to keep it shut. Heading over to the sofa, I held my head in my hands as I became sure he was going to strike me. It was then I decided to try to escape. I know now that William must have been coming down from cannabis; raging and violence are common at that time.

Later in A&E, I apologized to the nurse who cleaned me up, for not being able to stop crying. She said she understood. I'd had a terrible shock. She asked how old my son was, and I told her.

'You don't have to have him in the house, you know. He's 17. You can ask him to leave.'

I wasn't sure she was right, but I was glad of the sympathy, although it made me cry more. When I got home hours later, Will had gone. He had borrowed money off Jack and scarpered. We didn't see him for days after that.

I'd been sure, at the time, that it would be a turning point: that William had crossed an invisible line and would be so shocked by what had happened that we would be able to have a new beginning. How naïve I was, and how little I knew about addiction. I wasn't convinced you could even be addicted to cannabis, although I was aware that there were stronger strains available now to when we were at college. I had little understanding of the risks to mental health of smoking in teen years – only what I'd read in the newspapers. I just wanted our son to stop and for our lives to be peaceful once more.

It was after this that we had insisted that William go to counselling with us. We made an appointment to see our family counsellor, who we knew quite well, as both Will and Jack had been to see her – William about his phobia of injections and Jack after he had been mugged twice, which had affected his confidence. The counsellor was a woman in her thirties, of West Indian origin, working in an inner-city environment: I felt sure that she could help us in relation to our fears around William's cannabis use. But she admitted to me at the first session that she knew nothing about cannabis, and urged me to focus on other things that might be going on in our family. When I mentioned my hand having been damaged in the door, she also gently asked me when I was going stop mentioning it, so we could look at other things.

Three years ago. Things hadn't got better. There had been many false 'new beginnings', which really only happened in my own personal reality and in noone else's. We approach this Christmas estranged from our son, and with our extended family in tatters too. This is the first Christmas in the twenty years Guy and I have been married that we have not all spent Christmas Day together. But we cannot see how that could be possible this year.

My sister has always been understanding about William, and over the years has taken to calling him 'a little shit, because that is what he is', and her anger and support have been good for all of us.

Guy has continued to be superbly firm with his mother's attempts at reuniting us with William. 'We don't like having our strings pulled,' he told her most recently.

It was a mistake to tell her on the telephone last month – when she asked me what I expected from my son – that William should fulfill his promises after coming into a considerable sum of money.

I expected him to do what he'd said, I told her, as a gesture of recompense for the amounts he had stolen from us over the years. I'd told
her about his feeble excuses and expected her to sigh, and agree with
me that this was probably more lies. Instead she just said that she had
a cheque book. She also mentioned that she knew that Guy and I liked
apologies in writing. What did that mean, I wondered?

What is it with her? She comes across as an intelligent woman who
can talk about most subjects and appear normal. Why can't she accept
that Will needs to take some responsibility? It's surely obvious that we
don't want money, or anything material, from her. That's not the point.
We want Will to begin to put things right himself. We've told her this
repeatedly. What part of it is so difficult to understand? Christ!

Guy's birthday came. (Will's is just two days later). He left for work
before the post arrived.

I was happy to see a brown envelope arrive, with Guy's name on the
front hand-written by William. He had remembered his father's birthday. It was a thick packet too, so maybe a cheque *would* be in there.
That's great, I thought, we are getting somewhere. There were also
other cards too, one bearing his mother's writing.

Guy rang later to say he was on his way home. I told him, brightly,
about Will having remembered his birthday, feeling relieved that I had
good news about our eldest son for once.

'Is there one from my mother as well?' he asked.

'Yes.'

'Look at the franking on both of them. I'll bet they are the same.'

Sighing, I picked up both the letters to compare the stamps and
frankmarks, wondering why Guy should be cynical about this. Will had
remembered. That should be enough, shouldn't it? But both the letters
bore the same Kingston-on-Thames franking.

'They're both the same,' I said slowly and quietly. 'Posted in Kingston at the same time.'

'Sorry, Deb, but I know my mother too well. They probably all met
up in Kingston, my sister and Mum's old stomping ground. She'll have
stood over Will while he wrote it. I'm not going to open it. There'll be a
cheque in there but you can bet your bottom dollar that my mother's be-

hind it all. Will wouldn't do anything without her behind him. They've cooked this up between themselves. I'm not interested. '

'Oh,' I said into the phone, far away now, staring at both letters again, comparing the stamps, disappointment in my voice.

'I'll send it back to her. I don't want it,' he was saying.

That is what he did too. Alex opened the envelope later when Guy came home. There was a birthday card, a long well-written letter from William wishing his father a happy birthday and apologizing for being an awful son, and a cheque for £500 from a building society in Kingston, purporting to be from William but not drawn on an account of his.

'Seal it up again. I don't want any of it,' Guy said, slipping off his jacket and hanging it on the back of a kitchen chair.

We sang happy birthday and Guy blew out the candles. Make a wish! I could guess what Guy was wishing for.

He sent Will's letter to his mother the next day, with a type-written letter politely telling her to butt out: to give up meddling because we would never have Will back and that was that.

William rang the next day. He was with Grandma, he said. I could hear her saying something in the background. Here we go again. Had they got the letter back when they were both together then? How appropriate! Instant karma in action?

'Did Dad get the letter I sent?' Will sounded strong and upbeat.

Oh, it would appear they hadn't got Guy's letter then.

'You'll have to ask him.'

'I just want to know if he got the letter and card I sent him. Surely you know that ? With the cheque for £500 I sent? Ring any bells?'

'Look, I'm not getting involved. You'll have to ask him yourself.'

'Oh, well, okay, I will. I just want to know if he got it; that's all. Surely you can say? Anyway, I'm down here with Grandma. I didn't want to be alone on my birthday. My family doesn't want to know me... '

'So, do you have an address? There are birthday cards that have come for you and I can post them on.'

'No, I don't. I have moved, but I don't know the address yet.'

Come again? More fantasy from Will-land.

'I've got a necklace here for you. I'm going to leave it here with Grandma unless you'd like to meet up.'

'I'm guessing Grandma bought it,' I said. 'Will, do you think I'm stupid? I don't want it. I don't want to meet either. But have a lovely birthday on Saturday. Look after each other.' I felt my heart open as I said these last few words, really meaning what I said.

A necklace, eh? I told Guy later and he smiled saying that I needed to understand just how literally his mother will have taken my words.

'You say you want a cheque and a necklace, so she sorts it. More meddling.'

My mother-in law rang me later that day apologizing for upsetting me a few days before by asking for Will to come back and live with us. She obviously had still not got the letter that had been sent back.

'Look, let me give you some advice, Caroline,' I said. 'You are going to have to be more dispassionate about Will. You need to step back more, and be more of an observer, rather than getting sucked into his world and then trying to fix things here. Stop trying to save him because you can't do that; only he can save himself. There was an interview in the paper about one of the Rolling Stones who said he would have kicked his addiction long before, if he hadn't had people always trying to bail him out, and it's the same with Will. And there is no way that we can have him back. We have the two other children to look after and protect, don't you see that? You are also going to lose your own son if you carry on like this. I'm serious about that – listen to what I'm saying. You are going to lose your own son, and that would be awful, wouldn't it?'

I knew that the letter would arrive back on her door mat the next day, and wanted to warn her without spelling out what Guy had done.

I cried all day the next day in anticipation of Will's birthday, knowing that I had no intention of remembering it in the sense of sending him anything this year, nor of seeing him. He was going to be twenty. I was in pain about Guy's family too. It wasn't fair, my inner child was screaming. I had wanted a close extended family, and now we were in dispute, and not communicating properly – all over Will, who had chosen a highly destructive pathway.

Exactly a year ago, on Christmas Day at my sister's, Caroline had told us that her friends thought it was 'disgusting' that her grandson couldn't be with his family at Christmas. We had had Will back soon after, only to return to the chaos that had convinced us we should exclude him previously. She didn't have our family's best interests in mind. She wanted to 'paper over the cracks', Guy had told her, with no thought to the trauma that we had all been through – 'all' including three people who are her own flesh and blood, her son and two other grandchildren. It was hard to understand, and my pain at being estranged from my own first-born was compounded by this attitude.

Alex began to be ill again at the end of last month. He vomited at school, and I was asked to go in and bring him home. He has just moved up into the Middle School, which was where Will became exposed to cannabis and began smoking habitually. Alex was ill the next day too, and then said that he was sorry he had to go into school the next day.

'You're lucky, you can stay here. I feel safe when I'm here with you,' he said.

'Safe? How do you mean – that you don't feel safe at school still? They asked that boy to leave though, Alex – the one who was dealing cannabis in your year. At least they did that, thank goodness. The head of your year came to the House of Commons event too. That's an improvement. They are doing something about the drug thing, you know.'

I had talked to Alex's teachers earlier this year, when he was still in the Lower School (Year 8, which is for 12- to 13-year-olds), about Alex being offered cannabis by a young man in his year. Alex couldn't believe it, he said, that it took a 13-year-old to tell the staff what was going on in their own school. It was at this point, he said, that his respect had gone. However, I'd been happy that the school had acted quickly – lockers had been raided, and a stash of the drug was found. The dealer-boy's parents had been invited to remove him. I took this to be a good sign, and now Alex was expressing his unhappiness again.'Yes, well, I still don't think it's enough. Boys are bragging about dope, saying on the coach that they can point the younger boys in the right direction to get it. It makes me sick. School say they want to change things round drugs, but they don't. Just expelling that boy is not enough. They've missed out on really making a difference. So many of the boys are stoned there. It's a big competitive school, Mum, and I don't feel safe.'

I was standing in the kitchen, staring at Alex who was sitting at the kitchen table looking down at his hands as he spoke. My beautiful boy, who at 13 looked more like 16 – who made me tingle when he spoke, he was so articulate in the way he expressed himself. His unique gift. I remembered the effect he had had on the audience at the conference, back in October, and how many of us had had tears in our eyes as he had stood in Parliament telling his story of living with an addicted brother.

Taking the stairs two at a time up to my study, I emailed Alex's school immediately, reporting that the dope-smokers were in confident mood again it would appear, and warning them that I would be looking for an alternative school for my son, saying that history would not be repeated in our family. I reminded them that our eldest son's addiction had begun when in their care and mentioned that as a writer with an increasingly public profile, I might start writing about the school and its drug problems. Curiously, my colleague Mary Brett and I had been asked to go into the school to talk to the Deputy Master and the Head of Middle School about the possibility of giving a talk to the parents and boys. That had been a month previously. We were keen to do this but had heard nothing further. We had both begun to wonder where their manners were in not contacting us, even if it was to say they had changed their minds.

The Head of the Middle School had surprised me at our meeting by saying that they had an outside agency who was employed to come in and talk to the boys.

'Alex will have told you about it,' he said, turning to me.

'No, he hasn't mentioned anything,' I said, puzzled.

I later asked Alex about this company – Red Threads.

'No, we've had one 35-minute lesson on cannabis given by our PHSE teacher in the whole time I've been there. That's not enough.'

After the email I sent to the school, I was asked to go in to see the Headmaster as a matter of urgency. Good – I had a response. Alex, meanwhile, had become ill again and was at home. We talked some more, and I asked him how he would feel about not going back. He looked up at me and in his eyes I could see a brightness that hadn't been there for some time. For the first time he said that he'd like to leave and go to another school 'where I can be myself'. He had been resistant to changing schools up to this point. He explained to me that he had held back from getting too involved in anything at school because Will had been in the same house, and had been active and popular, and that part of him was worried that if he did the same he too would be pressurised to take drugs and then what?

'I'm surrounded by boys who all look like William,' he said, angrily. 'How can I work for my house to get the house tie when all I remember is Will wearing that when he was being such an idiot at home? You can see it in the eyes of the boys there – they are stoned and the school does nothing.'

We talked for a long time. I then began phoning other schools to see how the land lay. Alex said he wanted to go to a co-ed school. My sister, who had been a teacher, agreed that it was obvious that Alex liked the company of girls and even if that was the only reason he went to school, at least it was a reason. He had to start going to school, again, we both agreed.

Guy's and my meeting with the Headmaster of the school was unpleasant. Guy had warned me that it might be a 'charm offensive'. But this was more like a white-wash. We could sense a defensive barrier as we walked into his huge private office. The last time I had been in there had been for a meeting concerning one of the teachers who had been fired after 'debagging' boys on a field trip to France, which is public- school-speak for getting little boys to take down their trousers and run up and down corridors whilst others look on. Although William had been on the field trip that year, he had happily not been involved in the games. We were told that no damage had been done, and the teacher had gone. I reflected then that trauma often gets buried, only coming to the surface some years later. It never occurred to me then that two of my own sons would undergo rapid transformations at that school that would threaten our family's stability. The Head was in solemn mood. He told me that they were doing all they could, that their drugs policy was working and they were satisfied with that, despite my saying it wasn't good enough. One of his deputies was there with him; he looked uncomfortable. He was a pleasant man who had been present at the meeting that Mary Brett and I had been invited to in November about giving a talk to parents and boys. When I told them that Alex had no knowledge of Red Threads, the outside agency that I had been told was giving lectures to boys, and that he had only had one 35-minute class on cannabis, given by a member of staff, I was told that I must be confused. Red Threads was a future arrangement, and had not yet happened. No enquiry was made as to Will's well-being.

Alex never returned to the school. One positive from the meeting was that the Head agreed to waive the next term's fees if we decided to take Alex away. He had smiled then. So had I. I found Alex another school within two weeks. He's even done a trial day there now. A good friend of mine recommended the school to me – she said she could see Alex there, that her kids were happy there. We were in Greenwich Park walking our dogs on a freezing morning. I listened to her, and smiled, glad of her friendship. This was the same friend, another writer, who had recommended I pitch the *Cannabis Diaries* to the *Guardian* last spring. I followed her advice then – and look what happened! Without that, the Parental Action Group might never have been formed. She is an important guide to me, I told her recently, and she laughed, reminding me that she had also told me not to get a dog and I had done, and look what a great success that had turned out to be. I smiled, and said that she couldn't always be right but on two important occasions she had been.

Lily is now 10 months old. This will be her first Christmas with us and I've bought her a doggy stocking and a bone for tomorrow. I have no experience with dogs, but I knew that having her would be healing for all of us. I didn't know how, but I knew that it would be. She has helped me get over William. Having to look after her, walking her irrespective of what the weather is doing, has been good for me. She loves me with an intensity that I have not experienced since the birth of William, who as a baby was so close to me. I suppose having a baby is the nearest you ever get to being One with anyone, because for forty weeks you are just that – one.

The sadness of losing him has been healed. I now care little whether he returns to us or not. I'm too busy to care. The website has been a huge success. I feel I have a reason to do the work I am doing, because I know that it has helped so many other families. I look forward to the New Year, knowing that we have much work to do. As a group we are determined to do something about the misery that smoking cannabis can bring. I am grateful to William for the story that he has given me to write – without it I would never have begun these *Diaries*, and many people would still be in the wilderness, believing that it was somehow their fault that their children had begun to change. This is one of the things I wanted to do something about: it's not right that parents believe they are to blame, yet most do. To quote one father who wrote in after reading about our work in the newspapers: 'It's not us; it's the drugs, stupid!' The story continues to unfold, though. Last weekend Guy and I returned from Ireland, after celebrating a friend's birthday there, to find a letter addressed to William. Guy opened it as William has been told not to use our address for correspondence. It was a letter from a loss adjuster on behalf of Boots the Chemist. William had been caught shop-lifting at one of their London stores on 10 December, it would appear. The company was seeking to recover over £80 in damages from Will, separate from any criminal prosecution it said.

The next day I sent the letter back to them, explaining that Will no longer lives at this address and has not done so since last February. For a couple of days after I was close to tears almost permanently, angry and ashamed that my son was still stealing, that he is still causing ructions in the world. How dare he involve us too by using our address? One of my first thoughts, though, was to send a copy of the letter to Guy's mother, as proof that our decision not to have Will in our midst again was the right one. Putting her case for having him back to live with us she had said to me that he had changed, and she was certain he would never steal again, that he had put his past behind him. Well, clearly he hasn't changed, so we have had to do so instead. We are not seeing William, nor Guy's family, this Christmas. Festively wrapped presents have arrived. There is one for me from my mother-in-law. It looks as if it contains a box that might house a necklace.

Epilogue

18 months later
The road to redemption

We didn't see Will for over a year, and for all of us it is still hard to believe that this could have happened. With him out of our lives, though, our home became the haven it always should have been, instead of a place where you never knew what was going to happen next. We were able to find the peace we so urgently needed to try and move on as a family – Guy and me, Jack, Alex, and Lily, our cocker spaniel, who is now two years old. Lily has continued to be very important to our family's recovery. She makes us laugh, being both cuddly and loving, yet she's mischievous and naughty too. We have to take her out for a walk every day, which is healthy and distracting. So, a real success, and something I'd recommend to anyone who has suffered trauma and loss. You don't have to live with a broken heart.

Our first meeting with William after a year came about because, after the initial months of silence, I had begun to have some good telephone conversations with him. We never planned to meet. Will had begun to 'check in', as he called it.

I had passed on his mobile number to a few journalists, who had interviewed me and who I trusted, and who had expressed an interest in interviewing him. As a lobby and campaign group, and then later on that year when we became a charity, Talking About Cannabis received extensive media coverage. We were especially vocal in our push for re-classification of cannabis back to its Class B status, and the debate had been taken up with enthusiasm by the British media. Another mother, Rhianna, and I gave evidence to the Home Office *Cannabis Review* in

February that year. The Government had asked the ACMD (Advisory Council on the Misuse of Drugs) to look again at whether cannabis should be returned to its pre-2004 status. We argued that reclassification would be some small recompense to parents who were struggling with the daily real-life ramifications of the Government's decision to downgrade the drug. The law was finally changed, just as we had pressed for, a year later.

So, Will began to talk to the media. Interviews with both of us were published on the same double-page spread in the *Observer* in May, and by *Good Housekeeping* magazine in August that year. I was very busy doing numerous interviews, for newspapers, magazines, radio, and national TV and now Will's voice was adding to the urgent call to take skunk cannabis seriously.

Will phoned me one day when I was at the BBC, waiting to give an interview, sounding very excited about a photo shoot he'd just done for a freelance piece he'd been interviewed for. He told me he had been asked to be a spokesman for the Government website and helpline, 'Talk to Frank'. An interview with him was going to form part of their new website, he told me. What an irony. I remember ringing the Frank helpline when I was upset and madly looking for answers. The person on the other end didn't even know what skunk was! She had also said that it must have been a Class A drug Will was on, because cannabis didn't make you aggressive or violent. I put down the phone feeling more confused than I had when I rang.

Talking to Will about the TAC campaign, and how he could help by giving his side of the story, began to create a bridge between us. I would often phone him when in the woods walking Lily. Surrounded by ancient trees, many times galumphing through mud, and watching Lily run around excitedly, I would listen to his voice, hardly breathing so I wouldn't miss anything. I was aware of the changes in the way we spoke to one another now. We had something else to talk about: a common ground. He had become reflective about cannabis, and wanted to make sure other young people didn't throw their lives away for it. We talked for hours about what it had been like for him personally.

The interviews he gave to the press were about his search for redemption; his awareness of how his behaviour had impacted badly on everyone around him, particularly us, and how he wanted to restore his relationship with his family. Guy was quietly amazed when he read the proofs of the *Observer* piece. He had expected Will to blame us for what had happened to him, which had usually formed part of any conversation we had had with him. Now here he was saying something different, and I began to hope that William could turn round his life. I didn't dare to believe in an early reconciliation between us all. We had been through too much and we didn't want that anyway because the trust had gone. We were also all enjoying a normal home life.

The fact that the *Cannabis Diaries* had become well known, and that the media were taking a keen interest in them and the activities of the Parental Action Group, all helped our son to begin a slow recovery. He had rung me at first to ask if I could stop writing. But I didn't stop, and he said recently that one of the turning points was opening up the *Evening Standard* one day to see a double-page feature about himself. I had been interviewed about our experiences.

'In it I sounded like an archetypal drug addict, and I'd never seen myself that way before, and it hit me that that was what I had become. I'd never thought of cannabis as being harmful, and I stood by it for as long as I could.'

It became difficult to hide from what he had become. He told me that of the cohort of around sixty students at his school who had been habitual cannabis users, all of them had had breakdowns of one type or another.

We didn't have an address for Will, but mail had stopped arriving for him, so we had no need of one. He said he was living in south-west London and working in a pub. I continued to be unsure of the truth of any of what he told me, having learnt so painfully not to attach to anything he said. It might have been the truth – or not. I hoped for his sake that things were going well for him, but as you know, most of what he had told us over the past five years had turned out to be lies.

His calls to me became more interesting. In the autumn of our year apart, he began talking to me about having given up cannabis completely, which again I took with a large pinch of salt. But he sounded lucid, calm even, and deeply thoughtful as to what had happened to him. Talking about the effects cannabis had had on him, he focused on the physical effects. I'd usually talk about what I'd been learning about the mental health effects, but he told me that the final push for him to give up had come from his body.

'I felt like my body was going to give up completely. My stomach ached all the time. I couldn't eat. I was in pain almost constantly. And it was that that made me give up. I also had a permanent cold, and couldn't live a normal life – things like getting out of bed in the morning were impossible.'

I remember his stomach complaints – we had thought the problem might be linked to cannabis, but knew so little about how it could affect people that we could not be sure.

So, as his twenty-first birthday loomed when he rang me in late October, I talked about us meeting up to give him a present. He had rung to give me his new address, and Guy had seen this as a good omen – that William was making an effort to want to be in touch in a more legitimate way. Guy was going to be 50 two days later, so I talked to him about us all meeting to celebrate the two birthdays. I was still having to be careful how I talked to Guy about William as Guy would view it as a question of my loyalty to him. But this time, he said that if I wanted to see William, then he would come along.

I rang Will the next day, and asked him if he wanted to meet up between the birthdays. He sounded pleased and said that he had a present for his dad. Great! (But was it true?) Well, whatever the truth, I was happy at the prospect of seeing him again. It felt the right thing to do.

Jack was pleased too, though he had seen Will recently. Guy had always made a point of telling the boys that they should see Will if they wanted to; just because we were estranged didn't mean that they should be. Will and Jack had met locally to where we live; Will had bought Jack a meal, which we thought was a good sign.

'I was going to pay for the cinema too,' Will said on the phone when I congratulated him on his generosity to Jack. 'Jack had the tickets, got a discount or something, otherwise I would have paid.'

This was new. He sounded energized; a deposit had been placed in his personal integrity account, which urgently needed the funds.

Will hadn't sent anything for Jack's eighteenth birthday the previous April, so this must have been recompense. We all took this as a good sign about Will, and quietly hoped that there would be more of this.

I spoke to Will on the phone a few times before our meeting, asking him what he would like for his birthday, what he needed. Will told me he needed pots and pans for his kitchen, and mentioned again that he had something for his father.

'Well, I've got a cheque actually. Remember I was going to pay him back. Five hundred pounds would be okay, do you think?'

'Yeah, of course, great,' I replied, but feeling uneasy that this might all be fantasy again added, 'We have a present for you from the boys, and Joan too.' Joan was a friend of the family, who had always liked William, and had been a support to all of us over the years.

We met at Brown's in Covent Garden. It had been raining since the early hours, and didn't stop all day. Will turned up (always a chance he might not; we were all prepared for that). We had decided between us that we would wait half an hour and if he didn't show we'd have a nice meal anyway. But, there he was. Giving him a big hug, I automatically smelled his clothes – no trace of skunk; that was new. He looked tired, and pale, but he'd had a party to celebrate his birthday the night before, so that might have been normal.

Guy was quiet, saying little apart from a smiling hello to his son. The other boys were clearly delighted to see him again, and began chatting immediately. Jack later said, 'It's funny. Maybe it's because we're brothers – we just pick up where we left off, not like you could with a friend, I don't think.'

'We've got presents for you,' I said to Will, reaching down to get the first one for him. He opened them all, looking very happy, smiling and laughing.

I leant over to him a few minutes later, asking if he had something for Dad, as it was his birthday too. He said that he needed to talk to me about that and handed his father a birthday card.

Here we go again, I thought, more broken promises. Where was the cheque? Still no sign.

Epilogue

'This isn't right, William. You said you had a cheque for Dad,' I whispered to him.

'Yeah, well, I don't have a cheque-book.'

The other boys both looked at me and asked if I could just leave it.

'It doesn't matter,' said Alex, directly. 'I'm sure the best present for Dad is that all his family are around him. You're just making a fuss, Mum.'

'Yeah, Mum,' Jack joined in, 'Just leave it. It doesn't matter. We're having a nice time.'

None of them knew about Will's promises to me.

'I don't like being lied to,' I hissed at Will. 'But you can go and get him something – there's the whole of Covent Garden out there. You can go and get him something, can't you?'

We had begun eating by this time. I felt choked with anger that Will was lying again. Will put down his cutlery and left. And so did I. Angry and reminded of all the past times when he had promised things and then not delivered. God! I realized that I had believed he'd changed, and even that I was expecting to get the old Will back. He had sounded so normal on the phone all those times we'd spoken – what was this about? No cheque-book. I'd heard that so many times, and he was doing it again! The big band refrain 'After all we've been through' struck up in my head and I dashed into the Ladies to hold my head and cry. Guy had come after me, calling me, but I didn't want to talk to anyone and ducked downstairs.

The restaurant was crowded, umbrellas and wet floors everywhere. The toilets were crowded too. I barged into a cubicle and locked the door. A young mother talked loudly to her little daughter next door, do-ing the keeping-the-door-closed-with-her-foot thing I imagined. 'Come on, sweetie, that's it.' She sounded so full of hope and in control of things; how did it go so wrong with us all?

I had just sat down at the table again when Will returned soaking wet (he has no coat), gripping an M&S bag by its middle. He'd bought Guy a jumper. Grinning, Guy accepted it and seemed genuinely pleased. I could see Jack looking over at me, questions in his eyes. My face was puffy and red, my newly straightened hair was now frizzy after firstly being out in the rain and then close to my tear-soaked face. I avoided Jack's eyes, and wished I could just go home to Lily. Then I'd be okay, because this was too hard.

The boys and Guy began playing a movie quiz they used always to play when they were young, and I sat looking on, trying not to show how wretched I felt. Why had I thought things would go well, and be perfect again? He'd always been good on the phone, but meetings in person were often difficult. I needed to think, to get some answers. Get me home.

I knew I'd done the right thing, insisting Will go and get a present. The boys went shopping together after lunch, while Guy and I paid the bill and waited for them. Guy asked if I was okay, leaning over to take my hand in his.

We had offered to drive Will home afterwards, and he'd agreed, but once in the car with us he said he had to go to work and would we drop him at Waterloo station instead. I helped him get his presents out of the back of the car, and gave him a hug.

'Sorry about that,' he said, presumably meaning the birthday present issue.

'Okay. You did get him something, though. I love you, you know?' I replied, giving him another hug.

'You too,' he said, looking down, clutching his gifts.

He walked off in the rain, not looking back to wave. I began to worry about his having no coat. But that wasn't my problem anymore, I supposed. I had bought him a jacket the year before. I guess it must have been lost like so much of his stuff. I got back in the car and we drove off.

'I was wondering if we would have a good time after your row with him, Mum, but we did,' said Jack. 'It was good, yeah.'

I turned round and looked at my other sons, two wonderful young men. But how did we get so disconnected as a family? Oh, yes, that's right, cannabis came between us.

I was glad to see Lily when we got home, and pulling on wellies to take her out for a walk, I was aware again of what a help she'd been to me these past months. She was so glad to see us, mainly me, who is 'pack leader' it would appear. I realized how she'd helped mend my heart – always glad to see me, and always wanting to play. Just what I need.

Epilogue

* * * * *

At the end of January, two months after our meeting in Covent Garden, a journalist from *BBC Breakfast News* rang, to ask if I would be interviewed on film, about our family's story, for a feature to coincide with the reclassification of cannabis. After the findings of the *Cannabis Review*, the Government had announced that cannabis would be reclassified back to Class B. As a group we were delighted. As Director of the charity, I was asked to give a comment for the Home Office press release announcing the decision. A proud moment.

The BBC producer asked me if Will might be interested in giving his views too, and consequently both of us were filmed together at Will's new flat in Balham.

I hardly slept the night before. Experience had taught me not to trust too much where Will was concerned. I was unsure what I would say to the news crew if my son were not there, for example, and even if he was, I was unsure how the interview would go. This would be the first time we had done an interview together. Added to this, I had only been to Will's new place once before when he had invited us all, in early January, to go over and see it.

He had moved there late last December. He rang one night, just before Christmas, to tell me that he'd found the perfect flat through a letting agent (which would indicate he was working, because I know you need work references to rent through an agent). He was going to have to move out of the flat he'd been in for only a few weeks, the address of which he had recently given us. The agent had said he wasn't earning enough to keep renting it. A new property had been suggested. Not having had an address for him for almost a year, being told about his plans was something new.

'You wouldn't believe it, Mum,' he told me, excitedly. 'This house, right, the landlady lives in an identical house next door – she reminds me so much of you: young blonde woman with kids, and they've said I can have the flat. It's got wooden floors, and everything is brand new. Nice road, tree-lined, reminds me of home. I can afford it too.'

'Great! That's wonderful,' I said, smiling, pacing our hallway to calm my surfacing Will-jangled nerves. Looking down at the worn-out hall carpet, I made another silent wish that we could justify the money to replace it. 'This is your reward now, angel, that things are going your way. You've just got to keep on the right track, and everything will start to fall into place. Your story has helped so many people, and now it's your turn to have things the way you want them.'

'Yeah, I really hope so.'

We went on to talk about Christmas.

We had all been invited to lunch at my sister's house, in Dulwich, on Christmas Day. As you will remember, we alternate hosting the day between us – Guy's sister, my sister and our family. But things had been made complicated these past three years by William's exclusion.

After the birthday meeting with Will in November, Guy and I had had many conversations about what we were going to do for Christmas. It was our turn to host it. However, it was too soon to have Will in our house again; we all agreed that was out of the question.

Then my sister rang to invite us all over to her house for Christmas Day – including Will – which solved our problem. Guy would go over to collect William from his flat in Balham. Guy's sister and family would not be there – she and her family were spending their first ever Christmas abroad.

'You still okay for Christmas then, Will? Dad will come over to collect you and take you to my sister's.'

We talked for over an hour then, him saying that his best present this year would be the fact that his family wanted to see him again.

'You don't know what it's like living without your family. That's why I wanted to do the interviews with the media: 'cos if there is one boy out there who may be put off cannabis by seeing how it affected me, then I need to speak out. Imagine, there could be some 16-year-old about to get kicked out, just like I did, and I may be able to stop someone else from having to live without his family, which has just been the worst thing.'

Oh, God, things have been really tough for him. But he's coming through it, and says he is no longer smoking cannabis. I asked him what helped him through, got him to this point. I was surprised by the answer.

'The funny thing is, that I knew if I could just get back to where I was before all the awful things began, before cannabis, I would be okay. I was a success before; I know I can be again. And I've held in my mind the image of our house, knowing that if I could just get back there – like to the Holy Grail – I would be okay.

'I needed to try it on my own, though. I've made so many promises to you, to girlfriends, to friends, I needed to do it on my own first so I didn't continue to let people down. But, you know the main thing was your story. You had no parents, and look what you've become. I've never known your parents, although I feel as if I have; I can see when I close my eyes your mum and dad in my mind's eye. Those photos you have around the house seem to come alive then. And I've always thought about your life – you came from the North, your parents died when you were young, you've really suffered, and if you could do what you did – come to the South, marry a lawyer and get a new life – then the sky was the limit as far as what I could do.'

I smiled then, shaking my head.

So – all this work writing the *Cannabis Diaries*, setting up the website, the lobbying – and it was actually merely the life that I had lived, and the alchemic transformation from 'orphan from Morecambe' into Blackheath housewife and mother, that had had the most effect on William! Amazing. Maybe it is ultimately the life you lead, and who you are, that matters the most. Is that the blueprint for change? I'm beginning to believe that we have to transform our own selves first, before transformation in the wider world can take place. It sounds logical, and yet mystical, at the same time.

Christmas Day had turned out to be a good one, the best for years. William looked so happy to be with his brothers and cousin again. He had bought presents for everyone. He had rung me many times in the preceding weeks to ask what people would like, even calling me from Neal's Yard store in Covent Garden, to ensure he had the right product I'd requested. We all joined in the games at the end of the evening, and Will appeared relaxed and respectful of everything and everyone. The boys smiled and laughed together all day. A memorable Christmas.

The *BBC Breakfast* interview went well. Will was at home when I arrived there, which made me breathe easier. Taking off my coat, I spotted a sink full of dishes and quickly washed them up before the crew arrived. There was only one tricky, heart-stopping moment during the morning.

Will was interviewed alone first. He was honest in the extreme about how cannabis had affected his life, even admitting to stealing: he talked about how his 'moral lines had become blurred'. I listened in fascination; a lot of this I had never heard before, and I was stunned that he could speak so openly about such a personal matter.

Whilst I was being interviewed, Will went to sit in his bedroom, which adjoins the only living area – a combined kitchen, diner and living room. I went into his bedroom after I had finished the interview, to see Will sitting on his bed with my phone in his hand, and my wallet open beside him. I had taken change out to feed the parking meter, before doing the interview, and had left my purse ajar. Looking quickly inside, and at the credit cards still sleeping silently in their compartments, I could see the irony of the situation. Everything looked in order. Will must have seen the look on my face.

'I was just playing on your phone. Hope that's okay?' he said, not mentioning the purse lying open.

'Yes, of course,' I muttered, not looking at him, not quite believing I could be so stupid as to leave my purse open like that.

'It's all safe. I wouldn't dream of taking anything any more, you know,' he assured me.

I took him out to lunch afterwards, as we had planned, and then to the supermarket to buy groceries. I had been upset to find that his fridge and cupboards were virtually empty, and thought about our over-stocked kitchen at home. We then made a date for clothes shopping in the West End. When we had all met in November, Guy had been shocked that Will had no coat and had asked me if I would take him to buy one soon, which I was delighted to do. We met a few days later, after Will's first live interview on his own, at the BBC in central London, to buy clothes and shoes. I took him to my hairdresser's for a haircut too.

* * * * *

Will and I have done many interviews together since then, including *Woman's Hour* with Jenni Murray, and the *BBC World Service News*. Each time I hear him speak, I understand a little more about what his journey with cannabis has been like. He talks about how he began ('A boy in my class was selling it. I trusted my friends when they said it was safe'), what effect it had had, how he had managed to quit. I am becoming increasingly impressed by his courage and candour. We all are, apart from Guy's mother and sister, who will not talk about my work, or the charity's achievements, or the interviews Will and I have been giving. It is all ignored. They are ashamed of me, I think, for writing so publicly about our family.

As to us, we all know that by doing this work we have helped bring the hidden issue of habitual cannabis use among the young, out into the light. As parents you automatically blame yourself when things go wrong with your children, but placing blame anywhere is always unhelpful.

A friend recently described our story in interesting terms: he said it was as if an articulated lorry had come round a corner and run into our son, leaving him permanently injured. Although superficially that analogy seems to fit, what it takes away is the notion that taking drugs is an accident and not a matter of choice. Although downgrading, liberalization, the activities of the legalization lobby, and the consequent presence of drugs in our schools all contribute to our failing to protect our children – and this has to stop – drug-taking is still a choice. Parents who assume responsibility for a child's choice are similar to a person who jumps into a river to save someone who is intent on drowning. There is always the chance that by seeking to rescue someone who doesn't want to be rescued you may sacrifice yourself along the way.

Often drug users will point the finger of blame at parents. It is a common story. Whether you accept that blame is another matter. Good parenting is about nurturing and protecting the young, and when parents feel that they have failed to protect, then they often feel they have failed altogether, with all the damaging and destructive energy that guilt brings. The uncomfortable reality is that no matter what age the drug user is, ultimately it is a matter of choice whether to use drugs or not.

When drugs enter the equation of someone's life, a whole family can be thrown off balance. If an addict is looking for support and help to become rehabilitated, then a parent can be alongside offering what they can to help bring healing to the child. In our case, however, we devoted 90 per cent of our time for five years to trying to deal with Will, and did not spend enough time nurturing and protecting our other two children. We realized that there was a possibility that they would look back on their childhoods with a lack of affection, feeling that their needs had not been met because of one person dominating the scene.

Our attempts to put zero tolerance rules, and strict boundaries, into place ultimately failed to bring our son back from the brink of being made homeless, but they did limit the damaging effects on the family. To that extent they were successful.

* * * * *

It is now nearly two years since Will last lived at home, and just over 18 months since we let him go into freefall and regrouped as a family. We now have the beginnings of a good relationship with him – something we had given up on – which is cause for great celebration. It is not a perfect ending, but it is one of hope. We have adapted to the fact that Will's own particular pathway is just that – *his*. It is not one we would ever have chosen for him, obviously, but we have had to step back from thoughts as to what 'should have been', or who was right and who was wrong, and learn to accept what happened for what it was. As the Sufi poet Rumi wrote: 'Out beyond the realm of right and wrong there is a field; I'll meet you there.'

We felt a sense of failure when we had to tell our son to leave, but we were making that decision because of his behaviour and his choice to abuse drugs. Our quality of life improved almost immediately once he was out of the house. As you know, we did not throw him out on the streets; we were never able to go that far. We always made sure he had money or somewhere to go, usually both. He was always cushioned, and many would say that was not the right approach and he should have been forced to reach 'rock bottom'. But his own private 'rock bottom' emerged at the right time for him. As he has said in interview: 'If my parents hadn't done what they did, I'd be in my old bedroom still, eating white bread sandwiches, watching TV and playing on the Playstation. I wouldn't have moved on at all.'

He talks to me a lot about personal evolution. We have discussed that image of the butterfly having to emerge from its cocoon by itself. If you try to help it, it dies. It is the same for all of us maybe. The strength acquired by getting out of something that is enveloping us, is what is needed for the next stage in personal evolution. Without the effort, you don't build up the strength necessary for the journey. Nor do you connect with the inner personal wisdom, vital for achieving a meaningful life, which resides in the soul with which we are all born.

What we have drawn from our experience is that the entire family has to be considered. We wanted to keep our family intact, and that meant excluding Will. Within all of this we have also given our eldest son an opportunity to confront and take responsibility for his behaviour, actions and lifestyle, which has helped him effect the changes he so urgently needed to make. We have also, at the same time, ensured that our other children were able to live as normal a life as possible. They are both thriving. We all are. The decision to exclude Will has been the right one for all of us, including him.

Jack is now 19 and on a three-month trip to the US and Canada, with two friends he has known most of his life. He's phoned a few times, and sounded very grown up, grounded and calm. Alex, now 15, is six foot four, slim and very happy. His new co-ed school has worked out well, hence the transformation. He was able to begin again and 'be himself' as he had said to us when he finally gave in to the idea of moving schools.

William came to our house this week to see his grandmother, Caroline, who is now in her early eighties and has been staying with us for the past ten days. She fell and broke her right arm rushing for a bus on her way to the station to get a train. She had arranged to meet William in London; she had a bag of clothes he had left at her house when he was last there. She rang us from the hospital, and Guy literally dropped everything to drive down to look after her. He brought her back that night, and she has been with us ever since. Her face was badly bruised too, and she had a nasty gash above her eye. She had fallen in the street a couple of years ago too. We told her then that she should slow down. 'You make no allowances for age, Mum,' Guy had said to her.

I had been surprised then to hear her say, nodding: 'It's pride before a fall, you know. I'd been doing all my accounts, ticking off my jobs, and feeling very pleased with myself. Then I fell.'

I had taken the opportunity to talk to her about how competitive she can be.

'I think when there's no one else to be in competition with, you talk to yourself competitively, and set yourself tasks and time-limits. You need to slow down though, or you will fall again.' It had taken a lot of courage to say that; she is quite frightening at times. You never know quite what she is going to say, and she often begins praising herself, which can be wearing.

She had agreed with me about slowing down, though, and said she'd think about that. One of the first things she said to Guy when he located her in A&E this time was, 'Debra told me to slow down.' So, she had remembered. I was pleased. We had hardly spoken to each other for months. I had given up trying to be friends after we'd been so hurt by her attempts to have Will reconciled with us.

Friends have said to both Guy and me over the years, when we have mused about the lack of comprehension within his family, that unless you've experienced it you can't imagine what it must be like to live with drug addiction. Then you need to use more imagination, is my internal response, but I nod and say that's probably right.

With William and Caroline both at our place this week, I realized that this was the first time we had all been together in the house for years. Alex commented that it took an accident to bring us all together, as, smiling, he came into the sitting room with the Monopoly board and then told us all we should play, which we did. He had already played Scrabble that afternoon with his grandmother, echoes of what they used to do whilst at his grandparents' house during childhood holidays there. We ate in the garden that evening – the weather has been glorious – and it was still warm as the day ended. Will came with me to the supermarket that we hadn't been to together since our many visits there before his total exclusion. It brought back all those times – the two of us, when he was in B&B accommodation, and then in the rented house close by. We bought food for a barbecue, and Will and Guy cooked for everyone.

I wasn't there when Will arrived at our house for the first time in 18 months. He had told me the day before that he would almost certainly be over to see his grandmother, and us, but hadn't given a time. He still rarely talks to his father. If he rings the house he almost always asks to be put on to me. This saddens me, and I know that it hurts Guy. Two weeks ago Guy had rung Will to ask if he wanted to meet up on what turned out to be the day that Caroline fell. Will had said that he was due to meet his grandmother that Saturday, and Guy had invited himself along to see them both. Killing two birds. He had been getting ready to go when the call came from the hospital.

Guy was driving me to the station to get a train when I saw Will in the street, near the station, en route to our house. I was going into central London for a meeting, and was running late. I heard a voice call out 'Hey!' as we were driving along. Looking through the driver's window to my right, in the direction of the voice, I saw William standing still in the street, his hand high in the air waving to us, beaming, beanie hat on head.

'Will!' I cried out, and then heard my own voice and wondered why it sounded so excited. That invisible umbilical cord again. Okay, just calm down.

'Right, I better get back and lock the doors upstairs straight away,' Guy said, quietly. Going into close focus on Guy then, I could tell he was fine about that, just resigned to another job. How far he had come; you could never say that Guy was ever stuck. He's had to negotiate so many changes these past years, and is now in a very happy, contented place. For all of us there has been a grieving period which is now over.

Guy had been working at home so he could look after his mother, and was trying to do both things well – a precarious balance. Will had promised he would be over earlier in the week, when Grandma had first arrived, but had cancelled. Guy had spent half an hour collecting up cheque-books, jewellery and computer games to lock away, he said. I had been out that day too. Ironically, the day after Caroline arrived I had gone down to where she lives in Surrey. I had been asked to give an interview for the BBC local radio station, about the *Cannabis Diaries*. The whole thing had been set up weeks before. And now here we were changing places. I wondered what that could mean, not totally believing in chance.

Caroline is sleeping in the little attic room at the top of the house I use as a study. That was curious too. After making the bed up (there is a double bed in this room which is why she is up there, needing more space due to broken limbs – normally she sleeps in the single bed in the study), I began looking round the room. I tidied away things I believed she might not approve of, like my various packs of angel and goddess cards, crystals, nag champa and incense holders – some of the contents of my 'tool box' that I've created over the years to help me in every aspect of my life. Later I went up there to find a file I'd forgotten and saw her clothes hanging in the little wardrobe up in the attic room, next to jackets and dresses of mine that I can't fit into the wardrobe in our room. An odd juxtaposition given the distance that there has been between us these past years.

Alex remarked on how odd it was that I was going down to her town and she was here. We were both in each other's space, he said.

Walking round Guildford in the bright sunshine after the interview, I tried to tune in to what it must be like to have lived there most of your life. Married in their very early twenties, Guy's parents, who were both Londoners, had moved down to Guildford after the War looking for an attractive large town where they could settle. It had been an 'uneventful childhood', as Guy said to me once.

'How do you mean?' I asked.

'In the sense that nothing eventful happened,' he replied. 'Just the opposite to yours. As Oscar Wilde wrote: "to lose one parent may be regarded as misfortune; to lose both looks like carelessness". Crikey Deb, yours and your sister's lives are like something out of Dickens. But both of you are so strong. You have to be to have got through it all.'

He looked at me then in the way I love, with care and surprise on his face, and joy in his eyes. I told him I'm not sure about the strong thing, but yes we got through.

I wonder now whether Guy's mother must have been thinking it was my legacy that made Will go off the rails. She once mentioned to Guy that there were no mental health problems in her family, and that it must be 'on Debra's side'. Guy reminded her about a maiden aunt who had not exactly lived life at ground level, and she was quiet then. She hadn't mentioned cannabis, but Guy did after that.

A friend of mine also once said to me that Will might have inherited my father's genes. (He committed suicide when I was very small, as you will know if you have stayed with me during this diary journey.) I calmly changed the subject then, because I just do not believe that anything my father did could have been inherited. Having researched his life and death, I am convinced that his entire nervous system had become completely mangled by his RAF bombing experiences. Now it is called 'post-traumatic stress disorder'. Then it was treated with a nice cup of tea, and someone telling you to get on with your life, and how lucky you were to be alive.

'Yes, of course. Drop me here, then,' I said, as Guy talked about locking things away. He's right, we may never trust Will again. Guy kept driving though, until we got to the station. He turned to kiss me goodbye.

'Crumbs, Will and my mother at the same time. You're in the right place this afternoon. Don't hurry back,' he joked.

I smiled and wondered when we were going to get some peace in our lives. But that's not fair; we have been having a very peaceful life since we made the heart-wrenching decision to let Will go. Our lives are very busy, that's all.

There seems to be a coming together of us all, though. Caroline hadn't mentioned my work, the campaign, the media appearances, the charity, once during the previous two years. As if it had not been happening. When I was at an anti-drugs conference in Romania last year, giving a speech, she had rung. When Guy had told her where I was, and that I was speaking at an international conference, she had said, 'Oh, dear'.

'What do you mean, "Oh, dear"?' he had said to her, always quick to defend me.

'Oh, just that it might be too much for her, with the family and all.'

At Christmas Alex had been alone with her in our house, while we were out, and had talked about a recent interview I'd given for radio or TV. Caroline had said that it was 'something to fill your mother's day now you boys are growing up'. Alex had reported this to me, looking down as he spoke, and then up at me to look in my eyes and tell me how little his grandmother understands about what we've all been through. I know he is proud of what I have been trying to do. We have all been through so much, but it's made us close and anchored us in a way that might not have happened had we not had these experiences.

I think this has come through to Caroline these past ten days. Being vulnerable, with her right arm in a sling, and bruises on her face, maybe there has been an acceptance of what has happened. She has asked about my work, wanting to see some of the cuttings. She has been agreeing with me about the need to protect children from drugs. She seems genuinely moved by stories I have told her about the suffering of families. As Guy said to me yesterday, 'When the chips are down, she can see who stepped up to help her and maybe she's realized that, as Jon said to us that day, "we're quite nice people really".' (That was during the supper two years ago we had had with Jon and Julie Myerson, when we had talked about our struggles with our cannabis-using children, and how many criticisms were thrown at us.)

I've been angry with Caroline these past years for not supporting us, but I don't think she knew how. Her belief system, and consequent default mechanism, is that families must stick together, despite everything. This is what she learnt as a child, and has carried that lesson with her, even when it has meant that its application could be destructive and divisive. We have been telling her that William needed to take responsibility for his behaviour, and ultimately for his own life. She witnessed, this week, the relationship we still have with our son: that we can still welcome him back home, but need also to protect ourselves and our property.

The trust may never return. I don't know. But it was good to see Will. It occurred to me the other day that I have conversations with him that

I can't have with anyone else. I told this to Caroline when she began telling me how glad she was to see Will reunited with his family, and enjoying family time here with us. She had been concerned that she would die before seeing us all reconciled, she explained. Yes of course – the final curtain is about to come down yet the play's ending has yet to be written. She then said something quite extraordinary, given how much I know she adores William. 'He's very in touch with his feminine side. He's very like you, I think.'

Two Christmases ago, I opened the boxed gift that had arrived for me from Caroline, half-expecting to see a replacement necklace for the one I had been asking Will to supply. I had been relieved to see that it wasn't. Inside was a bright pink box of body lotion, with the words 'MIRACLE' written in large silver letters on the outside. I am reminded of that now. We have all come home as a family, and that really is a miracle.

APPENDIX 1

Some useful information for parents and cannabis users

Dr Zerrin Atakan
Consultant Psychiatrist/Honorary Senior Lecturer
Institute of Psychiatry, London, UK

What is addiction?

Addiction can be defined as continued use of a substance, despite experiencing its adverse effects, and inability to control its use. The person affected may start behaving in such a way that they would be prepared to do anything to obtain the drug they are addicted to. Addictive substances can cause physical and/or psychological symptoms when the person stops taking them or reduces their use drastically. If someone has such reactions to withdrawing from a drug, this would mean that they have become 'dependent' on it. 'Tolerance' to a drug means they come to need higher doses or amounts than originally in order to achieve the effect they want to experience.

Is cannabis addictive?

Cannabis used to be considered to cause psychological dependence such as 'craving', but not physical dependence or 'tolerance', even though some early research carried out in the 1980s demonstrated that chronic users showed withdrawal symptoms (Jones et al, 1981). However, later research confirmed Jones et al's findings, showing that humans can indeed develop physical dependence on cannabis, especially if they have become tolerant to it (Crowley et al, 1998; Morgan *et al*, 2009). As dependence relies on regular and heavy use, wide-scale availability of high 'THC' (delta-9-tetrahydrocannabinol) -content cannabis, such as 'skunk', has increased the risk of dependence.

After alcohol and tobacco, cannabis has become the most commonly used drug of dependence in Australia, Canada and the USA (Hall & Pacula, 2003). Chronic cannabis use is now considered to produce a dependence syndrome in as many as one in 10 users (Hall & Degenhardt, 2009). Research shows that if someone has behaviour disturbance during childhood or adolescence, is rebellious, is a poor academic achiever, has a poor relationship with their parents, or their parents have drug and alcohol use problems, they are more at risk of becoming dependent on cannabis (Anthony, 2006).

It is important to be aware that most teenagers do manage to control their use of cannabis while experimenting. On the other hand, becoming dependent on cannabis for some teenagers can take as little as 28 months from the first use, if used on a regular basis – a very short time compared with tobacco (3-5 years) and alcohol (5-9 years) (Blecha *et al*, 2009). In the light of this brief period, it is crucial that parents are aware of the early signs of dependence and are able to communicate effectively with their children.

What are the physical withdrawal symptoms in cannabis dependence?

Someone who has become addicted to cannabis can experience withdrawal symptoms within the first eight hours, following cessation, and these are more pronounced during the first 10 days. However, it has been reported that they may last for up to 50 days or more. The symptoms below are listed in the order of frequency, with those at the top being the most often experienced (Crowley et al, 1998; Morgan *et al*, 2009).

- Feeling tired, weak and sleepy and yawning a lot
- Feeling irritable and angry
- Having difficulty in concentrating
- Feeling low in mood
- Sleep problems: having strange dreams
- Poor appetite
- Seeing, hearing and feeling things that aren't there

- Runny eyes
- Sweating
- Increased heart rate
- Muscle pain
- Feeling sick
- Diarrhoea
- Tummy pain

It is important to be aware that these symptoms can happen due to causes other than cannabis smoking. Parents should not jump to conclusions immediately when they observe these signs. Establishing open communication with one's children and encouraging it from an early age is always considered to be helpful.

What are the warning signs of addiction to cannabis?
- Using more, or for longer, than was usual
- A constant desire to use, or trying to give up and failing
- Spending a lot of time getting supplies, using and recovering
- Spending less time on important activities or giving them up altogether
- Keeping on using, even when the harmful effects are well known to the user
- Tolerance (needing increasing amounts of cannabis to get the 'stoned' effect)
- Withdrawal (unpleasant symptoms when cannabis is stopped)

Can cannabis affect the development of young brains?
Human brain maturation begins before birth and continues beyond puberty if full functional potential is to be achieved in adulthood. Even though the mechanism by which cannabis affects the developing brain is as yet only poorly understood, there is growing evidence that the endocannabinoid system in humans is largely responsible for structuring certain central nervous system functions such as mood, cognition and reward mechanisms. Early interference with this natural process as a result of cannabis use is highly likely to affect development. There is

growing evidence in support of this hypothesis. For instance, research looking at the effects of maternal cannabis use on the fetus indicates that there can be structural changes in the fetal brain (Jutras-Aswad et al, 2009). Adolescent cannabis use can also lead to alterations in emotional and cognitive performance and may even lead to an increased risk of schizophrenia in adulthood in pre-disposed individuals (Realini *et al*, 2009).

What are the effects of cannabis on the body and the brain?
As cannabis receptors are widely distributed in the brain and spine and many other parts of the body, including the heart, liver, spleen, pancreas and reproductive organs, cannabis can have wide-ranging effects.

Effects on movement and motor functions:
After an initial mild stimulant effect on the central nervous system, cannabis use leads to:
- Lethargy
- Reduced fine motor control
- Reduced manual dexterity
- Reduced motor co-ordination
- Reduced complex task reaction time

Its effects on driving are:
- Cannabis impairs performance more on closed courses than in real traffic. One explanation for this is that users compensate for the impairing effects of cannabis in more serious situations
- However, there is an increased risk of road traffic accidents with cannabis use
- Effects of cannabis on driving are less than alcohol intoxication

Its effect on flying are:
- In studies with flight simulators, cannabis has been shown to impair the performance of experienced pilots even 24 hours after smoking it.

Effects on heart and vascular system:
- Dose-related tachycardia (increased heart rate); tolerance to this effect can develop with chronic use
- Vasodilatation (widening of blood vessels) producing, for example, reddening of the conjunctivae (whites of the eyes)
- Postural hypotension (sudden drop in blood pressure when standing up from a sitting or lying down position) and fainting
- Increased risk in cardiac patients
- Increased blood glucose
- Increased blood lipids

Effects on the respiratory system:
The cannabis plant contains similar constituents to tobacco, such as:
- CO (carbon monoxide)
- Bronchial irritants
- Mutagens and carcinogens

Note that 3-4 joints = 20 or more cigarettes per day.

Other effects include 'munchies' (craving for particularly sweet things), dry mouth, and stomach ulcers.

Psychological effects:
Psychological effects may vary within the same individual. The amount of THC in the cannabis used, the mood the person is in, the environment and who they are with can all have an impact on the effects.

Effects on mood:
- 'High' – the 'stoned' effect
- Feelings of intoxication (light-headedness, confusion, heightened emotions, feeling of wellbeing)
- Anxiety (decreased to severe)
- Panic attacks
- Alertness
- Sleep disturbances
- Depression
- Increased sociability

- Extreme suspiciousness, paranoia, hallucinations – psychotic symptoms

Effects on perception:
- Distortion of perception - that is, illusions: seeing or hearing things which already exist in the environment differently than they are; colours can be brighter or sounds may be heard more clearly
- Changes in perception of time and space
- Hallucinations (seeing or hearing things which are not there in reality)

Effects on cognition (thinking):
- Inability to focus attention on tasks, reading, etc
- Performing poorly in tasks
- Temporary, dose-related short-term memory impairment
- Inability to calculate mentally
- Alteration of associative processes (new or unusual mental connections)

References

Anthony JC (2006) The epidemiology of cannabis dependence. In: Roffman RA, Stephens RS, eds. *Cannabis dependence: its nature, consequences and treatment.* Cambridge, UK: Cambridge University Press, pages 58–105.

Blecha L, Benyamina A , Reynaud M (2009) Family management of cannabis in adolescence. *Archives of Pediatrics* 3 Nov (Epub ahead of print)

Crowley TJ, Macdonald MJ, Whitmore EA, Mikulich SK (1998) Cannabis dependence, withdrawal, and reinforcing effects among adolescents with conduct symptoms and substance use disorders. *Drug and Alcohol Dependence* volume 50, pages 27–37.

Hall W, Degenhardt L (2009) Adverse health effects of non-medical cannabis use. *Lancet* volume 374, pages 1383–1391.

Hall WD, Pacula RL (2003) *Cannabis use and dependence: public health and public policy.* Cambridge, UK: Cambridge University Press.

Jones RT, Benowitz NL, Herning RI (1981) Clinical relevance of cannabis tolerance and dependence. *Journal of Clinical Pharmacology* volume 21, pages 143S–152S.

Jutras-Aswad D, DiNieri JA, Harkany T, Hurd YL (2009) Neurobiological consequences of maternal cannabis on human fetal development and its neuropsychiatric outcome. *European Archives of Psychiatry and Clinical Neuroscience* volume 259(7), pages 395-412.

Morgan CJA, Muetzelfeldt L, Muetzelfeldt M, Nutt DJ, Curran HV (2009) Harms associated with psychoactive substances: findings of the UK National Drug Survey. *Psychopharmacology* Online first: November 25 2009.

Realini N, Rubino T, Parolaro D (2009) Neurobiological alterations at adult age triggered by adolescent exposure to cannabinoids. *Pharmacological Research* volume 60(2), pages 132-138.

APPENDIX 2

The parent's perspective – what we have learned through our experience and from families contacting our website

Debra Bell

One thing is for sure – 'skunk' cannabis is not the stuff today's parents smoked in college, and as a result has caused much confusion among families. As one recovering addict said: 'Skunk may not be Class A, but it has a Class A effect. I've done just about everything, you name it, but it was that stuff I couldn't handle. It completely messed with my head for days and I was hallucinating. It was awful!'

Parents report a lack of up-to-date information, even from the medical profession, which has sometimes contributed to poor outcomes for cannabis-affected children.

Appearance of cannabis

'skunk' cannabis: small green lumps, with a sweet-sour pungent smell (the reason it is called 'skunk', after the animal), usually in a 'baggy' (small self-closing plastic bag).

Resin: can look like a stock cube, or solid brown lumps which may look like liquorice.

Grass: takes the form of leaves, stalks and seeds.

All forms of cannabis are usually smoked – rolled with tobacco in 'Rizla' papers to make a 'spliff', 'reefer' or 'joint'. Hand-made filters or 'roaches' are made out of soft cardboard, often ripped from bus/rail tickets. Cannabis is often used in 'bongs', a glass-bowl pipe – sometimes using water – and can be eaten by adding to food.

Street names for cannabis include: Bhang, black, black leb, blast, blow, blunts, Bob Hope, bush, cheese, dope, draw, ganja, grass, hash, hashish, hemp, herb, marijuana, pot, puff, Northern Lights, resin, sensi, sinsemilla, shit, skunk, smoke, soap, spliff, wacky backy, weed, zero, Afghan, homegrown, Moroccan.

What to look out for

Some warning signs that parents and teachers have reported include:

- Blood-shot eyes, with dilated pupils. Cannabis causes pupils to enlarge (unlike heroin, where pupils go smaller). A sign of cannabis use is evidence of eye-drops, e.g. Optrex, in bags and pockets.
- Baggies (small self-sealing plastic bags) in bags and pockets, with pungent-smelling residue or substance (usually green), large (or small) cigarette papers e.g. Rizla, bus-tickets/soft card torn in shape of a 'roach'.
- Clothes have an unfamiliar, unpleasant smoky smell.
- Finding items connected to drug-taking e.g. bongs, pipes, matches, plant seeds or stems, small cardboard tubes, silver foil, blackened spoons.
- Burn marks on clothing, carpets, furniture and skin.
- Dark eye bags, grey complexion.
- Poor personal hygiene, looking dishevelled and dirty.
- Couldn't-care-less attitude.
- Asking for more money than usual, which goes quickly.
- Stealing, shoplifting.
- Truanting from school.
- School grades dropping.
- Lying, being disrespectful and challenging those in authority.
- Staying away from home for long periods ('sofa-surfing'), sometimes with no explanation, and secrecy as to where.
- New, older friends.
- Becoming precociously independent – attempting 'adult' ventures when still immature, sometimes putting the individual in dangerous

situations and at risk.
- Depression.
- Rigid refusal to take responsibility for actions, deflection onto others, yet feeling lonely and misunderstood.
- Paranoia.
- Hallucinations.
- Aggression, violence (appears to be linked to the come-down and from psychosis.)
- Assault.
- Trashing of property.
- Food cravings – 'munchies'.
- Stomach and digestive problems.
- Inability to concentrate.
- Lack of ambition, short-term thinking, unable to plan for the future.
- Panic attacks; becoming disorientated.

If your child or teenager is using cannabis, he or she may be getting supplies from another child at school – this is commonly reported by parents. Ask the school what its drugs policy is (possession and dealing), and what its drug education comprises – is it based on preventing children from beginning on drugs? (Most schools follow the present Government guidelines of giving children 'informed choice', based on the premise that children should be given the freedom to make up their own minds about whether they use or not, which can be a 'green light' to some children to experiment.)

Be confident – the school is in 'loco parentis' and most children begin their addiction at school. You may be able to nip things in the bud. See the Head to find out if teachers have noticed a problem and ask for support for your child. Get together with other parents – parent power works. Remember you are the clients. Find out as much as you can about drugs to empower you. The 1990s 'Just Say No' campaign in the US, spearheaded by parents, saw a steep fall in cannabis use among the young.

Often users have little sense of the consequences of their actions, and their behaviour may begin to be destructive to themselves and to those around them. Be aware that colluding with your young person over drugs is only going to help them slip into addiction more easily – be strong as early as you can.

How you can help
Prevention

- Cannabis is the drug most young people begin with, sometimes leading on to harder drugs, and the age of initiation is falling. There is even evidence cannabis may prime the brain for harder drugs, so prevention really is better than cure (there is no fool-proof cure for addiction).
- Educate yourselves and your child about the effects of cannabis on the brain and biochemistry; teach younger children before they become tempted to experiment.
- Talk to your child about the fact that cannabis is illegal and what it may mean if they get a conviction.
- Be aware of what the law is: cannabis is a controlled drug and is a Class B substance; the penalty for possession is up to five years.
- Most significantly for parents: impress on your child that if they possess or produce cannabis (or any other drug) whilst on your premises YOU could be arrested and charged. This includes use or supply at a party or gathering in your house. In other words, if you allow anyone to use an illegal drug whilst in your home you are committing a criminal offence.
- Don't be afraid to let your children know that you disapprove of illegal drug use – research as to what deters children from using drugs shows that parental disapproval is high on the list (as is the fact that drugs are illegal).
- Set firm boundaries and house rules and stick to them. You and your partner need to be together on this – children can divide and rule.
- All young people need a safe place at home. Wobbly boundaries create confusion for everyone.
- Teenagers especially need to know who is in control, and may kick against your boundaries, but this is normal. Stay calm.

Appendix 2

If you think your child is using drugs:
- Confrontation will almost certainly elicit denial; instead, act in a grounded, measured way. Psychologists advise naming what you believe is going on without being judgemental. (Remember that peer pressure may be strong.)
- Keep lines of communication open by taking an 'observer' position. Try using language like: 'It seems to me...' letting your child know what you are seeing but without judging.
- Try and time speaking to your child when he/she is not stoned.
- Try and get children to talk about their feelings and what may be going on in their lives. The more we hear them, the more they hear us.
- If you suspect that your teenager is smoking cannabis, the first step is to make your home a 'Drug-Free Zone' and preferably a 'Smoke-Free Zone' too – to avoid any confusion as to what is being smoked.
- Include the garden and porch areas in this too.
- Let your child know that if the house rules are contravened there will be consequences – decide what they are going to be and stick to what you say.
- Try not to make the consequences too dramatic – whatever you set up you are going to have to stick to, or there is no point. Start small, or you will have nowhere to go.
- Try to get a land-line number and address of where your child is staying overnight if they go on sleep-overs ('no number, no sleep-over').
- Check what your child's friends' families' attitude to drugs is – discourage visits to homes where using is allowed or a blind eye is turned. This can become increasingly important.
- Talk to their friends' families about your concerns; they may not be as up to speed as you are. Ignorance about the dangers of cannabis is common.
- Impose sanctions when you need to. If you don't the child may 'up the ante' to provoke a reaction, encouraging you to be firmer. Remember, children like boundaries. In the outside world very often

the message is 'anything goes'; firm boundaries at home help keep children safe.

- Don't neglect other siblings and partners by giving the drug user too much attention.
- A good tip is to ration the amount of time taken up by them – make an allotted time (say 15 minutes) when the problem is discussed or dealt with, then move on. (This is highly recommended as addicts can become all-consuming to a household.)
- Seek help from your local GP for yourselves and your child (but it's useful to know that most family counsellors do not have drugs training).
- Be good to yourself. Beating yourself up won't help, nor obsessing about the problem, but being kind to yourself most definitely will. Make sure you do something nice for yourself every day; timetabling into your diary helps. This is your life too.
- For a list of agencies and charities who may be able to help, see our website: www.talkingaboutcannabis.com

Photograph by Rebecca Reid

ABOUT THE AUTHOR

Debra Bell is a freelance journalist. She lives in London with her husband, who is a criminal barrister, and their three sons. She set up the website, Talking About Cannabis, in December 2006, where she published the online diary on which this book is based. She began her career as a presenter and journalist on BBC Radio, moving later into print journalism as a feature writer, but now devotes herself full time to raising awareness about the potentially damaging effects of cannabis on the young.